PLAN FOR PROMOTION:
advancement and the manager

PLAN FOR PROMOTION:

advancement and the manager

TOM WATLING

Cartoons by Mick Davis

BUSINESS BOOKS
COMMUNICA - EUROPA

First published 1977

© TOM WATLING, 1977

ISBN 0 220 66327 0

658.3

*This book has been set 11 on 12 point Baskerville.
Printed in Great Britain at the Alden Press, Oxford
for the publishers, Business Books Limited,
24 Highbury Crescent, London N5*

Contents

Part One

INTRODUCTION

1

Do Organisations Plan for Promotion?

Do firms plan for promotion? Or does it just happen? Maybe the law of natural selection will operate. Perhaps the right man for the job will be there whenever a vacancy occurs.

Then, again, he may not be. The evolutionary process may result in the death of the firm, because it is not one of the fittest. A major reason for the lack of fitness may be that a firm does just promote the nearest available candidate — the next in line.

In looking at some organisations, you might be forgiven for thinking that the importance of selecting the right people for promotion is not recognised. This would be superficial judgement. Nearly every organisation, nearly every senior manager recognises the importance of promoting the right people. The trouble is that it is easier to see the need than to satisfy it. In some smaller organisations, the boss recognises the need, but leaves the solution to be found when day-to-day problems are less pressing. The longer he survives, the worse the eventual problem becomes.

Some larger organisations recognise the problem, but find it too difficult to solve. They just promote people in turn, hence the well known system of 'Buggins' turn'. This has some outwardly attractive features. It is seen to be fair — in other words, each person who can still breathe has an equal chance of promotion when his turn comes. It avoids the nasty business of choosing between people. It is easy to explain and it has a sort of logic. In a non-competitive setting, organisations that adopt this system can survive for a long time. The only snag is that if the best people rise to the top, it is incidental.

The modern, fast changing world calls for a positive approach to finding and promoting the right people. This is true not only of the commercial and industrial firm but also of the vast government and public sector organisations that are a feature of the modern industrial state.

SHOULD ORGANISATIONS PLAN FOR PROMOTION

Many organisations of all sorts and sizes do treat promotion planning as a serious matter of top management concern. Many have effective arrangements for selecting the managers of the future and for preparing them for their future jobs. Others seem to be taken by surprise every time a manager retires, dies or leaves. New management jobs, which arise from the firm's expansion, reorganisation and development plans arrive apparently so unexpectedly that top management's reaction is to look outside for the people to fill the new jobs. They reach for a head-hunter or take great spaces in the heavy Sundays to proclaim their need. Some know no better than to react in this way. Others excuse themselves on the grounds that the firm is short of management material and 'you can't make a silk purse out of a sow's ear'.

The mark of the truly great leader in any field is that he can leave his place in an orderly fashion. He has selected his replacement and has gone to the trouble of preparing him to take over the job. The transition from one man to the next is achieved apparently without effort. This is true not just at the top but throughout all levels of a hierarchical structure. The good manager at every level tries to identify his successor and coach him for the day he takes over. In practise, it may not be desirable in a large organisation for each manager to be succeeded by someone from within his own section, department or division. It may be, and probably is, desirable to have some interchange between the parts of an organisation so that they do not become too inbred. This requires that managers at the lower levels identify people for promotion rather than people specifically to succeed them.

Something more formal than just earmarking a replacement for each management job holder is needed. Every organisation requires a promotion plan. For small organisations, it may be sufficient for the boss to have thought about it. For organisations of any size it is necessary to develop a formal plan for promotion. Organisations that have existing, well developed plans may find it worth reviewing them from time to time. In that review, I suggest, they should go right back to the basic philosophy on which their plan rests.

WHAT SORT OF PEOPLE?

The most basic question is what sort of people do you want to manage your organisation. To answer this it may be necessary to go back to the nature of the organisation itself and to consider its objectives. In detail, the requirements of different management jobs in an organisation will differ and call for different characteristics, training and qualifications. There is, however, one very basic question to ask about the people: Who will run an organisation? What is it that will motivate them to do a good effective job? In considering this question, it is important to start at the top because the attitudes of the top man in any organisation are likely to be reflected throughout his organisation.

Popular belief has it that the motivation of top men in the public service is the desire to exercise power and to enjoy the outward symbols of authority. In the private sector, and to an increasing extent in the public sector, there is a theory that top men will only perform well if they are given very high rewards and perquisites. The prime motivator is seen as 'a slice of the action'. What is seen at the top as a legitimate carrot to persuade top managers to give of their utmost and to produce effective results may be seen differently by both work people and shareholders. They may be seen as greedy rapacious individuals in search of a fast buck. The people in the organisation may become convinced that top management are interested not in the ultimate success of their organisation but in the short-term maximisation of their own rewards. Worse still, if the carrots are designed to attract the man who is motivated by the opportunity to amass unusually large material rewards, the organisation will probably attract such people to the exclusion of others. It may be, of course, that your business or organisation does need a grasping self-seeker at the helm. It may be that reason for your organisation's existence is so lacking in any appeal except money-making that you have to have someone at its head whose real motivation is profit. If personal profit is linked to corporate profit, then all is well.

Lower down the management tree, it is common to preach that money is not everything. To obtain sound motivation you have to provide a job, which is designed in such a way as to satisfy the incumbent. In designing promotion plans and systems you should consider how top and other managers are to be rewarded. Maybe an effective structure can be designed that does not require an enormous differential between the managing director and first-line supervisors. Maybe we need to search for motivation systems that will allow us to find managers who will enjoy managing for its own sake rather than for the incidental rewards that are attached to it.

The promotion plan should also provide for a structure in which a man can step down or sideways without loss of face. It is common to think of 'face' as being an oriental characteristic. It is important as well in the West. Once people have been seen to rise to a certain level in a hierarchy, they do not like to be seen to be demoted. Given the Peter Principle that we are all eventually promoted to the level at which we are incompetent, this can lead to serious organisational constipation. Promotion plans must provide a mechanism for clearing those who have reached their level of incompetence. By that I do not mean that promotion plans must have a well developed firing mechanism — merely that there should be a suitable organisational arrangement that allows those who find a job beyond them to move gracefully to a job that better matches their capabilities even if this means moving down the hierarchy. The greater the difference in external appearances between hierarchy levels, the more difficult this becomes. Salary itself is something that can be allowed to take care of itself, but the continued use of a chauffeur-driven car and other outward symbols of status may be more difficult. It may be necessary to remove these symbols as the man is demoted and the fear of this loss and the associated loss of face may be what makes a man hold grimly onto a job he neither enjoys nor does effectively.

A well designed promotion plan and structure should give as much attention to keeping people moving downwards or sideways as it does to moving people upwards. The fact that a man can not do one job effectively does not necessarily mean that he is incompetent at everything he touches. The man who performs hopelessly at director level may have been an excellent department manager and would again make an excellent department manager if he could be returned to this level without complete destruction of his self-respect and confidence.

PROMOTION AT DIFFERENT LEVELS

A promotion plan is not just concerned with planning to fill the top layer of jobs. Modern organisations have a whole hierarchy of supervision and management posts and the promotion plan is concerned with the filling of all these posts. Furthermore these posts are not just staging posts on the way to the top. At each level a significant number of people will reach their ceiling. They will not be promoted further. It is important that they should be well suited for their job and that a training programme keeps them up to date and suitable for retention at that level.

Whenever it is clear that a manager is not performing satisfactorily and is a candidate for demotion, a confidential review system should come into use. This should try to identify the reasons for non-performance and see whether anything can be done to retain the man at his present level. If a demotion has to be made, serious consideration must be given to taking the opportunity to provide additional training.

A characteristic of large modern organisations is that they contain a large number of specialist staff appointments that are filled by individuals with particular knowledge or skills. They may perform a key function in the organisation and yet never manage more than a secretary and a couple of assistants. It is important that any promotion plan provides for these people. Their value to the organisation lies in their special knowledge and skills. They should be promoted in such a way that their rewards can rise for continuing to use those skills and that knowledge. The promotion plan must avoid the trap of offering specialist staff the choice between continuing in their speciality at a lowly level or moving into a management/administrative stream. The top-class scientist, systems designer or lawyer is far too valuable to the organisation working in his speciality. He must not be lost to become a faceless administrator. This calls for a number of parallel promotion paths leading to a plateau at a senior level rather than a sharp pinnacle at the top of a single ladder. Such ladders tend to be based firmly on administrative posts, where the greatest weight is given to the man who manages most people.

This principle should apply to all specialist streams, not just the prestige ones — although the top plateau for some specialist skills may be lower. Thus a highly skilled draughtsman should be able to obtain promotion to a senior position without undertaking the supervisory duties connected with running a large drawing office.

A major problem in many organisations is that a high proportion of their management jobs are filled with people who have neither the aptitude for nor real interest in management. They are in the jobs because the management route was the only one offering them the standing and rewards they wanted. A sound promotion plan guards against this and is concerned with putting each person in the job where he is of the greatest benefit to the organisation.

PEOPLE CHANGE OVER TIME

It is commonly thought that people who get on in life put their head down when they enter school and keep doggedly pursuing their career from that point until they reach the top. Many large organisations appear to build their promotion plans on this premise. The managers of the future enter the organisation at a certain level and then are put over a number of hurdles on their way to the top. The man who falls behind in the early stages frequently stays behind. Such organisations generally have some well publicised examples of people who make it to the higher ranks from among more lowly entrants. They have had to keep their nose permanently to the grindstone in order to climb successfully up the extra rungs at the lower level of the ladder.

Two important factors are often overlooked in the design of a promotion plan. First, the fact that people's attitudes change over time. Second by the fact that people who have devoted their time too exclusively to their work and to progressing up the ladder can become stale, narrow in their outlook and out of touch with developments outside their immediate concern.

In some ways people's behaviour follows a consistent pattern over their lives. Society is organised in such a way that the drunk, the gambler and the womaniser tend to become set in their ways. The man with two criminal convictions is probably set for a life of crime. Yet among the mass of ordinary people, attitudes of the individual do change. The extent to which those changes in attitude can be reflected in changed performance is constrained in many ways by society and in particular by the structure and promotion plan of the organisations in which people work

Some people graduating from university or polytechnic or completing their professional training feel they have reached the pinnacle of success and rest on their laurels. Others feel that after so many years of hard effort they are entitled to some break during which they can enjoy some of the fruits. Many people put their work low on their priority list during their early working years. They are concerned with having fun, finding a spouse or pursuing a hobby. At work they are often more concerned to do work that interests them or allows them to travel rather than with a career. Among my successful manager acquaintances is one whose teenage activities were criminal and several who spent their early working years with enjoyment high on their list. Attitudes change with maturity and as family responsibilities increase.

In the academic field, the Open University was founded to give a second chance to those who, for whatever reason,

failed to acquire the academic education they were capable
of acquiring. This was financed by the Government, not as
a sheer exercise in philanthrophy, but to develop the country's
human resources. Any company's promotion plan should also
provide for the late starter or late developer.

The staleness of the man who devotes himself mainly or
exclusively to his job is another matter. Something can usually
be done about it by a mid-career break. The man's horizon is
forcibly lifted by a period of training or by a time in a
different type of job. Either of these courses can be adopted
in order to jerk people from their rut. The company's
promotion plan must allow this to happen.

ORGANISATION PLANS

Plans for promotion should be conceived to cover the whole
of an organisation. It is not sufficient for each separate division
or department to have their own plans. This is not just for the
sake of the individual. It is also for the good of the organisation.
Some organisations make it a rule never to promote a deputy
into his boss's job and always insist on moving people on
promotion. Hopefully, they enter their new domain on
promotion not just full of the keenness of the newly promoted
but also faced with problems that are new to them. They
arrive with no inbuilt prejudices in favour of the *status quo*
and may well produce useful new approaches and recognise
new opportunities.

An additional benefit of a policy of moving on promotion
is that the middle and senior layers of managers develop a
wide knowledge of the organisation's ramifications. They
are also able to build up a widespread informal network of
contacts throughout the organisation and this can prove of
immense value.

Yet another benefit in certain organisations, where security
is of paramount importance, is that the new manager comes
to his job without ties. If integrity is slipping or security being
compromised he may be in a better position to rectify it than
if a local man is promoted.

*When a vacancy occurs, they reach for their
cheque books and buy in the talent*

WHERE HAVE ALL THE GOOD MEN GONE?

There are some managers who perpetually moan about the
difficulty of finding good people to promote. They lament
the lack of able people in their organisation. When a vacancy
occurs they reach for the cheque book and buy in the talent
that some other organisation has taken the trouble to develop.
Managerial talent will not just develop itself. Potential
managers for all levels need to follow a path in which they get
suitable management experience and are able to make mistakes
without ruining their confidence and bankrupting their firm.
Their promotion path may follow any one of many different
routes but their progress needs to be monitored and they
need to be coached along the path.

A well developed promotion plan not only ensures that an
organisation has a well developed supply of talent ready for
promotion to fill vacancies as they occur, but also that it is
a strong motivating factor for people within an organisation.
There is nothing more demoralising to the management and
younger staff of an organisation than to see whole armies of
new men being recruited from outside to fill every senior

vacancy and every new management job.

This book is about promotion plans. I consider them from two view points. Part Two of the book is devoted to looking at promotion planning from the point of view of the organisation. Part Three looks at it from the individual's view-point. Chapter 2 provides an introduction to the individual viewpoint.

2

Can You Plan Your Own Promotion?

The simple answer must be 'yes'. It may be difficult and like other plans it may go wrong. Robert Burns wrote in his poem *To a Mouse*

'The best-laid schemes o' mice and men
Gang aft a-gley,
And lea'e us nought but grief and pain
For promised joy.'

None the less, we have a better chance if we plan than if we do not. Still, Burns had a point. In planning, it is sensible to recognise that things do go wrong. As Sam O'Donovan put it in his famous law: 'If things can go wrong, they will go wrong — and at the most awkward time'.

The answer is not to abandon planning but to approach it in a professional manner. Individuals need to plan their own careers and their own promotion with just as much care as a successful company planning its operations. As we shall see in Part Three, this does not mean that you enter working life with a forty-year plan that inevitably leads you to the top of the pyramid. That idea is certainly likely to lead to 'grief and pain'. A much more flexible approach is needed so that you can adapt your plans to successive changes in the environment in which you work.

Planning is not just a matter of deciding you'd like to become managing director or writing a few notes on a piece of paper. It is a process that requires a considerable amount of time and thought. A plan, once made, is not cast in concrete. It should be subject to continual review and revision to take account of new opportunities or obstacles. The business of planning is discussed later in Chapter 13. The point I would like to make here is that it does take time. A great deal of any manager's time is taken up in planning for his organisation. It does not seem unreasonable to me to devote 5 per cent of one's working time to furthering one's own career. At times you will spend a much high proportion of your time; for instance when you are on a training course. But week in week out, you can probably use 2 hours in every 40-hour week to planning and developing your career. A later chapter deals with that important resource — your time — and how you should concentrate it on important matters. One of the most important, to you, is your own career development.

When an organisation enters a new project, it plans the project carefully. It sets out its objectives, evaluates the risks, counts the costs and estimates the rewards. The individual must do the same in planning his career. It is, however, important to keep one's career in perspective. It is important to recognise that career may not be all of life. The man of average intelligence, who has sufficient determination, can reach the top of most pyramids. Even poor education and a comparatively late start can be overcome by determination, although shortage of time may then make the very top layers of a pyramid innaccessible.

NOT EVERY ONE WANTS TO GET TO THE TOP

In recognising that it is possible to get to the top, it is sensible also to ask: What is the cost? Is it worth it? If nothing in life will satisfy you but reaching the top of a large public company, public corporation, or government department, then you will feel compelled to strive for it. Most other aspects of your life will have to take second place to your career. The struggle to get there will be all absorbing and no doubt in itself interesting and rewarding. The pinnacle itself, once reached, may prove less satisfying. It may be that you feel that the costs in terms of the affect on your family life and interests are too great. In any case, it is a fairly sound rule to keep

*Avoid any open declaration to your boss that
you are not interested in promotion*

your options open as long as possible. You should avoid any
open declaration to your bosses that you are not interested
in promotion. They will probably take you at your word. In
this imperfect world, it is probably wise to pretend to a keen
interest in promotion, even if it is not particularly close to
your heart. Even if you have no desire to get to the top of
the pyramid, life may be a lot more interesting and rewarding
if you move a few layers up from ground level. The successful, thrusting growing company is always on the lookout for
fresh opportunities to exploit. It does not embark without
thought on new projects to take these opportunities. Even

though it may do so very rapidly, it does compare the alternatives open and carefully evaluates the risks and rewards. You should do the same. In the course of a lifetime there are many opportunities you can take or you can miss. Some people say that it is a matter of luck as to what opportunities come your way. Others say that the lucky ones make their own opportunities. Either way, the ambitious man should examine developments, not just in his own department but in the wider context of the organisation he works for and the world outside it. Each development should be considered to see whether any opportunity can be identified for your personal advancement.

INDEPENDENCE

Sometimes when opportunities do appear, people feel unwilling to accept them because the risks are too great or because they do not have the money to tide them over a transitional period. If one is to have flexibility and feel able to take necessary risks in order to advance one's career it is desirable to have a degree of independence. Some people have a natural independence of mind and willingness to back their own judgement. In most of us it is not that great and we feel the need for a boost to our confidence in the shape of adequate resources to enable us to face a period of no income or low income with comparative equanimity.

I am a strong believer in creating a degree of financial independance for oneself as early in life as possible. It is not necessary to become a millionaire, but it is a great morale booster to know that you own your own house even if it is mortgaged to a building society. It helps to know that you have no short-term debts or hire purchase and that you have an emergency fund available in the form of savings, which can cover your normal expenses for a few months if this is necessary.

I believe that it is important for any man or woman who hopes to progress up the promotion ladder to learn something about money and how to use it. Every successful manager knows about and uses money in his job. There is no excuse for not developing that knowledge and learning how to use it to the benefit of his own finances. I am not suggesting that he learns to commit fraud against his firm but rather that he learns to use his own money to the greatest possible effect.

In reading this book, I hope the keen ambitious man or woman will not skip Part Two. This shows you something of the way your employers may think about promotion and there is always an advantage in seeing how the other side think. It is worth considering what the bosses are looking for when they select people for promotion.

In some routine jobs, they may well be looking for cleanliness, punctuality, consistent attention to work and so on. I do not denigrate these important qualities. However in most jobs — and this is particularly so as you move up the ladder — they will look for results. Management by objectives has been all the rage in many organisations for some years. This means that your boss should be looking not for any random results but for some quite specific ones. He will be looking to see how far you meet your objectives if he has spelled them out to you. Additionally he will be looking to see how far you have contributed to enabling him to meet his objectives.

WHAT CAN YOU CONTRIBUTE

It may help to illustrate this point to recall an experience of my own. Some years ago, I had to assemble a small team of four people to complete a specific task in the period of a year. This was the development of a small computer-based system for a customer of the firm I then worked for. At the end of the year we were dispersed to different jobs within the company for which we worked. Arthur was a pleasant steady chap. He worked normal office hours and did what he was told to do, no more and no less. At the end of the project he got a small rise to keep his salary in line with the cost of living. So far as I know, he is still working for the same company at the same level and is most unlikely to see any promotion in the future. He just plods steadily on. Bill joined the team because of his specialist knowledge and his specialist contacts. He made use of this knowledge to good effect. He always warned me in good time if he thought we were doing, or about to do anything, that in the light of his specialist knowledge would be unwise. He made positive suggestions to improve our work and took pains to understand the work being done by the rest of the team and to learn something about their special knowledge and techniques. On leaving the project he was promoted and has moved upwards steadily since then.

Charlie also joined the team because of his reputed knowledge and experience in a specialist field. He was more experienced than the other three and was intended as my informal deputy. He knew all the buzz words and always enquired about objectives and deadlines. If he had a task to complete by a certain date, he always reported completion by that date. Inspection of the work frequently demonstrated that it either had not been completed or that it was done so badly it had to be done again. Despite the fact that the project was a very small one involving only five of us in total, he was never able to see his work in the context of the whole project. He produced virtually no ideas that contributed to the successful completion of the project and apart from getting done those tasks for which the presence of a 'body' was neccessary, was virtually a passenger. He was a pleasant enough man, but did not hit it off with the other three members of the team and although he had my backing was unable to achieve any success as team leader during my absences. This was partly because of his attitude to excercising authority. He became very peremptory and felt the need to make it obvious to the others that he was senior to them and in charge of a particular task. Not unnaturally he put their backs up and got little co-operation. We were several months into the year before I appreciated how poor a selection I had made in taking on Charlie. I judged that because Doug and I both worked hard and effectively, we could still complete the job on time and that it was better to carry on with Charlie. He would do some work and it would have taken a considerable diversion of my effort at that stage to offload Charlie, find a replacement and induct him into the job. Looking back on the incident with the benefit of hindsight and the wisdom of greater age, I believe this may have been a rationalisation. I was probably too soft-hearted — and perhaps afraid of the unpleasantness that comes with sacking or transferring some-one because they are not up to the job. Needless to say Charlie saw no promotion at the end of the project, notwithstanding its success. Over the years his position has declined relatively though he has avoided disaster by moving from job to job every few months, within a large group. The fact that he is a bachelor and willing to go to the less pleasant parts of the world on behalf of the group has helped him to survive.

Doug was altogether different from the other three. He was much younger and very inexperienced. He was better educated than the rest of the team with a good honours degree and a higher degree. He worked extremely hard, was full of ideas and contributed significantly to our success. He frequently missed his deadlines, but this was due to his enthusiasm for packing more into a task and devising more effective solutions to satisfy the end-user of the computer system. Missing deadlines is, of course, a serious fault but I was able to correct for it in preparing the project schedules and was in any case close enough to the work to avoid it causing serious difficulties. Doug had a further weakness. Once he had completed a task, he resented having to go back to it in order to rectify faults or make changes. However, the positive contributions he made to the work far outweighed his weaknesses. I was able to obtain a salary increase for him in the course of the project and to ensure his promotion after it.

I have written at some length about this little project because I believe it illustrates a number of points relative to promotion. While doing the bare minimum job and keeping your nose clean, as Arthur did, may ensure a rise through one or two levels in a civil service type organisation, it is disastrous in any more dynamic organisation.

The successful pattern is seen in Bill and Doug. Both had their limitations but both went out of their way to do everything they could to make the project a success. I made sure that the firm rewarded them for their contribution.

Their promotion has continued in the following years. I am sure that is because they bring their minds with them to the job and make a positive contribution to any organisation they work for.

Arthur demonstrates an approach, which can positively guarantee that its followers will never reach the heights. Arthur did — and does — only what he is told to do. When he comes to work he appears to leave his mind and his interests at home. He makes no contribution and consequently has had a whole series of dull, routine jobs, which reinforce his boredom at work.

Charlie illustrates another important point. In a modern industrial society, no man is an island to himself. He depends for his success in obtaining the co-operation of others. This is particularly true of anyone who hopes to progress up the management ladder. Charlie at that time — and since — has alienated his juniors by throwing his weight about and 'pulling rank'. Those who hope to progress must learn something of the art of influencing people and of leadership. Management is not a matter of telling other people what to do. It is a matter of motivating those who work for you, however temporarily, to make the best contribution they are capable of and of influencing those level with you or above you in the hierarchy to cooperate with you and adopt your ideas as their own. If you find you can not get co-operation from others, then you should consider as a matter of urgency why this is. If you can only come to the conclusion that it is because other people are bloody minded and uncooperative, then I am afraid there is little hope for you in the promotion stakes. You must look in yourself for the reason. In particular you should always be prepared to modify your own approach if it is not producing results.

One of the things you may find out as you climb the lower rungs of the ladder is that there are not enough hours in the day to do all the things you want and need to do. A common approach is to work longer and longer hours. However, after a while this merely produces diminishing returns as you gradually become staler and more work-centred. At the heart of the manager's job lies the business of resource allocation. There is never enough time to do everything and so the first resource that a manager has to learn to control is his own time and energy. Chapter 17 is devoted to this important matter.

MASTER OF YOUR OWN DESTINY

Certainly in your early and middle years part of your time must be given over to self-improvement. Time must be spent in developing your own talents and skills as well as your own knowledge of the industry and firm for which you work. This is not necessarily a matter of attending courses of instruction. As we shall see, a great deal in the field of management can be learnt on the job, particularly if you have the right boss, who is prepared to coach you.

To make your way up the promotion ladder, both determination and planning are needed. But however careful your planning, there is more to it than dry-as-dust calculation. People and your interaction with them are a key factor. I believe that the way in which you deal with people is the key factor. Your relationship with the person who at any particular time is your boss is a matter of critical importance and I discuss this at some length in Part Three. But other working relationships are important. It is common to find junior managers who go out of their way to establish good relations with their seniors yet do not bother about their equals or juniors in the hierarchy. This is a bad mistake.

There are some who hold the theory that productive results only come from abrasive relationships. Some Americans in particular seem to believe that results can only be obtained by breathing down peoples necks and threatening or abusing them. I believe in the direct opposite. Everyone has their good points and most people will produce of their best in an environment in which they feel trusted and feel that the value of their work is recognised. In the past tyrants have frequently been successful. Most organisations in the modern industrial world do not lend themselves to producing results by tyrannical methods. Results have to be produced in more civilised ways. Part Three is based on the philosophy that in the long run you will move furthest up the promotion ladder if you can carry other people with you — the people who work for you, your colleagues at all levels in the other departments and your own boss. Planning, quantitative and scientific techniques are important. But the central factor in management is people. The man or woman who wants to get ahead must learn how to handle people. You can't give orders to people who do not work for you. Yet the people who do not work for you may be the ones you most need to influence.

Part Two

HOW TO PROMOTE PEOPLE

3

A Policy for Promotion

'We have been impressed in our survey with the sheer frivolity
of the employers' approach to the selection and training (and
retention) of managers.' Thus wrote the author of the
Association of Scientific Technical and Managerial Staffs'
(ASTMS) booklet, *The Case for the British Manager.* He
might well have added promotion to his list.

Most firms, except the very smallest, have a policy for
promotion. In many it is not described by so grandiose a
title. Like the British constitution, it may be unwritten.
There are those who muddle through as the need arises and
those small firms who don't have a policy at all — the top
man just worries about it sometimes in the middle of the
night when he can't sleep or has a pain.

In medieval times there was little problem in planning for
promotion. Sons succeeded their fathers. Medical science
was at a stage where sons had, broadly speaking, to be
reasonably fit in mind and body to survive. Thus if you took
the precaution of procreating enough sons the succession
was provided for. If you were sufficiently powerful and
wealthy and your wife was unable to produce a son, then
you could set about producing them on the wrong side of
the blanket.

Medieval practice continues in some backwaters of our
society. In the main however, we are grouped into large
organisations — powerful, continuing bureaucracies of
industry, commerce and government service. To these

organisations promotion is not a simple matter of automatic succession of the first-born son. Nor is promotion policy limited solely to the problem of the succession. Even the succession itself is not just a matter of keeping the seat at the top of the pyramid filled. There is the question of succession to every job in the organisation that lies above the basic grade. Nor does the modern organisation have just one basic grade, through which everyone enters. People enter the modern organisation to fill many different specialist grades from cleaner to electrician, taxation specialist or architect.

Promotion policy must be concerned with expansion, contraction, change, equal opportunity and recruitment and motivation. It clearly impinges on industrial relations, on relations with trade unions and even on relations with foreign governments.

However, succession is still the first concern of promotion policies. Succession is fundamental to the survival of any organisation. If a manager is run over by a bus one day, there must be someone to carry on his job as soon as possible. Preferably this should happen smoothly without a war of succession with the losers in the contest either departing to other jobs or retiring on the job.

If a manager has been doing his job satisfactorily there should be no urgent need to fill it the day after he leaves. He should have the job well enough organised for his deputy to run it at least for a while. However the deputy may well not be the right man to succeed.

Some companies have elaborate succession plans with as many as three generations of successors nominated for each management job. It looks marvellous on paper and engenders confidence in continuity in the bureaucratic mind. However, the only such plan I have ever observed in action was not very effective. It kept managers and personnel managers busy preparing it for several weeks. However there always seemed to be a good reason why it should not be followed when it came to the pinch. The plan was eventually quietly shelved.

Plans for succession need to be more flexible. There should always be plans to cover the absence of any manager. However the final filling of his job is another matter. Any company which plans to expand needs both an inventory of its existing management manpower and plan to meet the requirements of expansion. Indeed both expansion and contraction must be considered. Some firms have regular plans for an annual intake of graduates or of management trainees. If the volume of such recruitment is based on a certain rate of expansion then there will be discontent and wastage if the rate of expansion, and with it the need for additional managers, drops.

Management, so it is said, requires the same qualities and knowledge whatever the business. It may be true at the top levels where an understanding of people and money are the prime requirements. Lower down the tree, some hard work, specific knowledge and experience is normally necessary for the effective manager.

It follows therefore that a firm planning to diversify must, as a key part of that plan, provide for the necessary managers for the diversified part of the enterprise. Many diversification operations prove very unprofitable because this aspect of the plan is ignored. It may also be that every top manager needs to know something of the industry in which he operates and of the environment surrounding it.

A promotion policy may be used to provide a spur to better performance. It can provide examples to encourage the young up and coming manager. It can provide a carrot to motivate him. It can also be used as a stick to beat him with. There can, as we shall see later, be dangers in a policy which puts too much emphasis on the importance of promotion. A most important aspect of any promotion plan is the effect it has on the motivation of the workforce — in particular the managerial work force.

BE SEEN TO BE FAIR

If a promotion policy is not fair and seen to be not fair, it will have an adverse effect on motivation. In extreme cases it will have an effect on the quality of staff you can recruit and keep.

Consider the case of the family firm, whose top jobs

always go to the family — however competent they may be. Anyone joining or remaining in that firm must recognise that he can never reach the top echelon unless he marries into it. One could of course argue that a Wealth Tax and Capital Transfer Tax is going to change that. Most people do not however look that far ahead. If the family are seen to be firmly seated in all the top jobs, good managers and potential managers will steer clear.

A family cabal at the top is not the only way of having an unfair promotion policy. Promotions may in fact be biased in a particular direction. It may even be right in given circumstances for this bias to exist. However you must recognise the impact this will have. In some organisations, promotions indicate that it is necessary to be an engineer, an actuary or even an accountant to get on. Less defensibly it may be that a public school education, a degree or skill on the golf course are a key factor in gaining promotion.

In some organisations the key to promotion to the top jobs may lie in having had one's early training in a firm that is thought to have been a particularly good training school. Such cliques may originate from Ford, Unilever, Shell or even Univac.

Similarly promotion may appear to go in a significant number of cases to members of a particular club, or a secret society such as the Masons. It may appear that certain religious or political views are a prerequisite for promotion. Worse still it may seem that certain views or membership of a particular trade union are an absolute bar to promotion. Similarly there may appear to be prejudice against women as such, or against certain minority groups in the population.

It is not sufficient for the chairman of a public company to mouth or write platitudes about people being the company's greatest asset and the opportunities which the company offers to all of them. The methods of selecting people for promotion need to be public knowledge and need to be felt and seen to be fair. If a man fails to be promoted into a job, his colleagues should feel that he was given a fair chance — even if he, himself, cannot see that this is so.

As a general rule secrecy breeds suspicion. It follows that if a policy of openness about matters affecting promotion is adopted, there is likely to be a greater degree of acceptance Those who see the system working and feel that it does not offer them much hope will leave for more attractive prospects. However, that is preferable to retaining them under false pretences to become a focus of discontent and frustration.

Methods that help engender a feeling of fairness include the internal advertising of all jobs in an organisation. If the requirements and qualifications are clearly stated, anyone who feels himself to be qualified can apply for the post. If also the person who is selected for the job is known to meet the specifications advertised, then this goes a long way towards meeting the requirement of being seen to be fair.

A system of annual appraisal is another aid to making promotion systems seen to be fair. Under such systems each individual is reported on annually, his performance and future potential assessed. Such a system has existed in the armed forces for years and is now widely adopted in the private sector. The proper handling of appraisal and staff reporting systems is a key aspect of any organisation's promotion policy and is discussed in greater detail in Chapter 8.

INTERNAL PROMOTION VERSUS EXTERNAL RECRUITMENT

A central question in any organisation is the extent to which jobs should be filled by promotion from within or by external recruitment.

If an organisation does not look after its staff, pay them properly and provide them with decent conditions of service, it is possible that the more able will leave the organisation to find more attractive prospects elsewhere. If an organisation does not take care in the selection and training of its staff, it may well find that through its own incompetence it has no one suitable to fill managerial vacancies as they arise. It is not an uncommon weakness to look at the people who work for you and to feel that they are really not quite up to it. In a way it is a form of vanity for a manager to believe that his subordinates will never be able to do his job as well as

*It is not an uncommon weakness to look at
the people who work for you and feel they
are really not quite up to it*

he does it himself. Thus some companies provide no
management training at all and plan on external recruitment
to fill most of their managerial vacancies. At the other
extreme are those organisations who plan to fill all their
jobs by internal promotion. In late 1961, the Personnel
Officer of a large UK company wrote of their policy 'I am
sure you will understand that we make it a policy to do the
majority of our recruiting in the age range of about twenty
to twenty-eight, and by this means we hope to train up
within our own business those who are competent to fill the
senior posts. It is very rarely possible for us to take in
somebody older than this, and it happens only in the case
of men skilled in techniques of which we have no previous
experience within the business.' This is a policy that has
considerable advantages. It provides a strong motivation
factor for staff in the firm. It provides a useful selling point,
when the firm is recruiting among the under twenty-eights
and presumably enables it to choose from among the better
qualified of that age group.

Whenever an older person is recruited from outside a firm to fill a management job, there is a danger that however careful the selection procedures you may make a mistake and recruit someone unsuitable. He may prove incompetent or may just not 'fit in'. Even if he does prove satisfactory, it will take some months of induction before he can pull his weight fully. The process of recruitment and induction is expensive.

Yet to be sure of being able to fill all senior and middle manager vacancies by promotion implies that an organisation maintains an adequate pool of potential talent to allow for natural wastage and some who just don't make the grade as well as those required for promotion. It also implies accurate forecasts of expansion and contraction.

An organisation that is steadily expanding and promoting internally can usually, other things being equal, maintain a high quality of staff in its junior jobs, spurred on by good promotion prospects. There are however some snags to a policy of total internal promotion. Organisations become set in their ways and develop traditions. There is an absence of fresh ideas and competition, which would come in with some external recruiting. Internal politics strengthen. Future promotions can be foreseen and counted on. It does not take much bad luck for all internal promotion organisations to head for complete inflexibility and eventual ossification.

There is a strong case for avoiding both extremes. The aim should be to make a high proportion of promotions from within but to make a point of recruiting at least 10 per cent of managers for medium senior and top posts from outside the organisation. It may be desirable to welcome into those 10 per cent of posts, those who started with the organisation but have then gone elsewhere for several years to broaden their experience. They will be particularly well placed to understand the strengths and weaknesses of the organisation.

A FUNCTION OF PEOPLE MANAGEMENT

People are the most important asset of any organisation. Napoleon I wrote 'In war, moral considerations account for three-quarters, the balance of actual forces only for the other quarter'. Napoleon knew more than most about motivating those who worked for him. Successful organisations are those where the people who compose them have a faith in the organisation and are committed to it — in fact those organisations whose morale is high.

Promotion policies have a considerable impact on the attitudes of people to the organisation for which they work. They help to set the tone of an organisation. They help to determine whether the bright and able stay or go. If an organisation is slow-moving, ponderous and unwilling to take risks, some part of this can probably be traced back to promotion policy. Conversely the organisation that reacts quickly and positively to fresh opportunities does not do so by accident. Some part of this attitude is traceable to the organisation's promotion policies.

Promotion policy is a key part of the people management policy of an organisation. There is no one policy, which is always and inevitably right. What is right for a labour-intensive retail organisation may not be right for a capital-intensive process control industry. What is right in a research establishment may not be right for a bank or government clerical office. However, many of the basic considerations are the same. In the following chapters we set out to explore the factors that should be considered in forming your promotion policy.

Every organisation should have a clearly defined promotion policy. This should be known not only to those administering the policy but to every person in the organisation. Clearly a junior clerk or lathe operative does not need to know the policy in detail. He should be aware of its basic principles and be able to find out simply and easily what prospects are open to him and what he needs to do to obtain promotion.

4

What Are You Looking for?

When you look for someone to promote into a particular vacancy, what are you looking for? When should you look?

A published succession plan has many drawbacks and elaborate company-wide succession plans are often an expensive waste of time and paper. Nonetheless, it is sensible to consider on some formal basis the potential for promotion — if any — of each member of an organisation. It is also sensible for each manager to consider each of the jobs whose holders report to him. If the holder dies or resigned tomorrow what would the manager do about it? Would he fill the job at all? Or would he reorganise so as to eliminate the need for the job? This is not as foolish a question as it may seem. It has been estimated that in a typical large organisation you could line up all the supervisory and managerial staff and arbitrarily sack every second one. After a period of hiccup, the organisation would function more effectively. Managers would be forced to act as managers. Less time would be wasted in company politics and swapping memos. Meetings of five managers will normally dispose of a given amount of business in less than half the time it takes a meeting of ten managers. This emphasises the need to think carefully before any promotion. You may argue that inefficiencies should be eliminated as soon as they are recognised. Organisations should be kept slim and efficient at all times. This is, however, to ignore the human and morale aspects. Many managers shrink from the turmoil of cuts that are not forced on them.

They prefer to carry on comfortably as they are. The man who should get the push may be a personal friend of long standing. However, the same considerations do not apply when a vacancy occurs.

DEFINE JOB REQUIREMENTS

It is common tenet of modern management that each job in an organisation should be clearly defined. Each job is specified so that both the job holder and his boss know what the purpose of the job is. The job holder's key tasks, targets and resources are defined. This enables a manager to make an objective assessment of his subordinate's performance.

One task of a manager is to ensure that the job requirements of his subordinates are drawn up in such a way that he fulfils the requirements of his own job. He will naturally specifically review them at least once a year. However if a vacancy occurs among the jobs reporting to him, he should immediately review the requirements not only of that post but of every post reporting to him. Organisations are dynamic, not static. Apart from the possibility that the job may not be necessary at all, changing circumstances may offer an opportunity to cut up responsibilities to a different pattern. It may be that you want to alter the responsibilities of the vacant post so that it is filled by an entirely different kind of person, maybe even by a person with certain specialist skills.

In all organisations, indeed in all societies, there are vested interests in the existing order. There is a built-in resistance to change. This is nothing new. Machiavelli wrote in *The Prince* many centuries ago: 'There is nothing more difficult to carry out, nor more doubtful of success, nor more dangerous to handle, than to initiate a new order of things.'

Thus, opportunities for relatively painless change should be seized. Whenever a post becomes vacant take the opportunity to review and if necessary rewrite the requirements of the post. Any manager should also keep the matter under review. The case for change may not be strong enough in the normal way, but he should keep in mind the changes

34

that it would be desirable to put into effect when a vacancy arises.

If for no other purpose, job specifications should be established for every supervisory and management post, as part of the organisation's promotion policy.

GRADING PEOPLE AND POSTS

I have already noted the dangers of an organisation becoming inbred and inflexible. In large companies it is not unknown for rivalries, jealousies and lack of understanding to grow up between departments and divisions. Marketing grows to think that Manufacturing are not trying, that Field Maintenance are inefficient and that Development Engineering have no understanding of user needs. Manufacturing believe that Field Maintenance are overpaid and have no idea how to treat lovingly built equipment, that Marketing are overpaid, congenital liars and given to making impossible promises. And so it goes on.

One partial cure in large organisations is to make a point of moving managers from one part of the organisation to another. Transfer or promote a manufacturing manager into field maintenance. Even try a marketing manager in manufacturing. This may seem heretical but it can work. It is particularly desirable to do this with people being groomed for the top jobs in an organisation.

For this to be possible it is necessary to have a system of grading posts across the organisation. People, similarly, need to be graded. This not only enables cross-company transfers and promotions to be made, it also helps, if done well, to establish a feeling of fairness as between one department and another.

It is important not to allow grading schemes to become too elaborate with dozens of neatly graduated steps between shop floor and chairman's office. The management principle of a limited span of control has been responsible for many extremely steep hierarchical structures of this sort. Yet the flatter a hierarchy is, the better and quicker communication normally is.

Another cause of multitudinous graded steps in a hierarchy is the alleged need to provide a system of graded steps up a progressive salary scale to maintain motivation. In fact it is possible to relate pay to people and maintain motivation without the need for an elaborately graded and labelled hierarchy. Indeed, if the number of formal levels in an organisation is minimized it is possible to move someone to a more responsible post without formal promotion. If he does not make the grade, he can be shifted easily into a less responsible job without the trauma of demotion.

This is particularly important if you accept that there is at least some truth in the Peter Principle that 'in a hierarchy every employee tends to rise to his level of incompetence'. A fairly small number of formal levels permits the employee who has risen to his level of incompetence to be redeployed into a job at which he will be competent, without demotion or loss of self-respect. It is not just in the mysterious East that 'face' is important.

More adventurous promotion policies are needed. People must be promoted while they are still young. As people with a comparatively short track record are promoted, there must be a risk of making mistakes and promoting people who are unsuitable or not yet ready. It is, I believe, worth taking these risks. But the company promotion policies must make it possible to rectify the mistakes without destroying the person concerned. They must provide a framework that allows him to be moved away from the job, which he is not up to, and into a job which he can do. If he develops later on or if some other avenue of promotion seems more suitable, this removal or demotion must not have been such as to destroy his self-confidence or self-respect. Few people have a career that is an unmitigated success from start to finish. Promotion policies and the related grading systems should allow for this.

Salary scales need not have a one-for-one equivalence with points in the formal promotion ladder. There can be a range of salary scales covering a given hierarchical level and the salary scales can overlap. This is of importance in rewarding people who are good at their job but who lack management or supervisory skills.

CHARACTER AND ACHIEVEMENT

There are those who contend that character is the supreme quality to be evaluated in selecting people for promotion. In a way this is no doubt true and always has been. The problem is how you judge a man's character? How can you tell whether he has got what it takes to accept responsibility and manage his department effectively so that it makes the contribution expected of it — or more?

There is a lot of truth in the old saying that the proof of the pudding is in the eating. You will only tell if he is up to the job when he does it. However, this is not much help in the selection process. For this you need some indicator that it is at least probable that this man is the right one to select.

I believe the best indicator of future performance is past achievement. There are some people who appear to be constitutionally unfitted for responsibility and who are incapable of bringing any undertaking to a successful conclusion. The main characteristic of these people is that they always have a good reason why things went wrong. They rationalise to a point where they can not recognise their own faults and weaknesses. The failure is always due to external causes. Otherwise, failure may be put down to ill health or to a mental breakdown.

There are, of course, some cases where failure is due to ill health or external causes. These are less than is generally claimed. In addition, if one is harsh, the qualities needed for successful achievement include foresight and political sensitivity.

Thus, in evaluating people for promotion, a most important aspect is the evaluation of their achievements. It is clearly easier to do this for someone who has been in an organisation for some time. You are able to gather together a more complete set of evidence than you can for someone new to the organisation. You can look back at the objectives he has been set over the years and the extent to which he has achieved them. You can probe the extent of the success or failure. You can try to establish the extent to which he has created his own opportunities.

Even with all the internally available information, it is

sometimes difficult to assess the extent of an individual's achievement. In large organisations many achievements are the result of a group or team activities and it is sometimes difficult to determine who provides the real motive force It is not always the nominal leader. Yet it is sometimes naive to put Mr A's success down to the fact that he has been supported in every successful project by Mr B and Mrs C. They may be extremely able and hard-working. They may have the technical knowledge which Mr A himself lacks. Nonetheless Mr A may supply the magic ingredient that makes the group successful. No one man is perfect. In a small group working effectively together the weaknesses and lack of knowledge or ability of each member of the group is covered by the strength of one of his colleagues. The fact that Mr A, on promotion seeks to pull Mr B and Mrs C after him into his new role is not of itself bad. It is not mere nepotism, but the recognition of the fact that he produces his best results with the help of the team with which he is used to working.

There are however some dangers to be recognised. The leader of such a team may not be the catalyst but a mere passenger who has found himself in position from some fortuitous circumstances. The second is the danger of a chain reaction following a promotion. Mr X is promoted to general manager of a different division. Within six months Mr Y and Mrs Z replace the Chief Engineer and Chief Accountant of that division. In the words of Dean Jonathan Swift 'A flea hath smaller fleas that on him prey'. So Mr Y and Mrs Z no doubt have their own small professional groups, which they like to have around them.

In assessing achievement it is therefore essential not only to identify whether it is actually the achievement of the individual concerned. It is also desirable to assess whether it is genuinely an achievement of a group as such, dependent upon the particular composition of that group. Some people have the knack of gathering a successful, well balanced group around them. They can do it time and again with different groups of people. Others can do it once and then become completely dependent for their successful achievements upon continuing to work with that particular group.

The successful group leader can be promoted without fear of disruption. The one specific group joiner may cause a trail of subsequent moves, some grossly unfair in their impact on individuals. This may have shattering effects on the morale of an organisation. It may still be right for an organisation to promote the specific group joiner. But the full consequences need to be thought through.

There is a further problem with past achievement as a forecaster of future performance in another and more senior post. The motivation and success of someone at his work may be, and frequently is, rooted in circumstances outside the working environment. The man who has overcome every obstacle in the past, who has turned every problem into an opportunity for greater achievement, may when those circumstances are destroyed, cease to perform. This may become immediately obvious. Alternatively, and more dangerously, it may result in his dropping into neutral and coasting along on the efforts of his subordinates. A promotion, which involves moving to a different place and working with different people, may result in disaster. It is not just that the man has been promoted to his level of incompetence; his motivation has been destroyed and unless that can be rekindled, he will be a problem to employ effectively not just in his new job but at any level.

This may well be a significant factor in the poor performance of many British organisations. A man, whose motivation fails in middle life, continues in office and may even continue to be sucked upwards in the promotion stakes. This happens because of the existence of strict, relatively inflexible, hierarchical structures combined with the concept of individual loyalty. Not only is there individual loyalty but also the necessity for senior men to stick together. They prefer in too many cases to allow a passenger to be carried rather than set a precedent of drastic downgrading or firing. This is one argument against allowing too much security of tenure.

Another aspect of this is that a man who realises in middle age that his organisation has 'passed him over' and that there will be no further promotion, can sit back. He can sit back, protected by his security of tenure, and do only the absolute minimum necessary to avoid disciplinary action. He is thus carried comfortably on to retirement, automatically benefiting from any general salary increases. This is perhaps a greater danger in the Civil Service, nationalised industries and educational establishments than it is in private industry and commerce.

Nonetheless, any promotion policy should be devised so that it does not completely remove the promotion stick/ carrot at too early a stage. A man who retires on the job at forty may be an expensive passenger for a quarter of a century. The biggest cost is not his salary but the effect on his subordinates and colleagues and above all the cost of the opportunities for his organisation which he allows to slip through his fingers.

QUALIFICATIONS

In considering people for promotion, great weight is some-times given to paper qualifications. This is particularly so when consideration is given to recruiting people from outside an organisation to fill a senior vacancy. In a way paper qualifications are seen as evidence of achievement and almost as a certificate of competency. This is all very well when recruiting very junior staff. There may be little other evidence of achievement to go on.

For appointments to senior posts, qualifications should be looked at with a degree of scepticism. In any case a mature man in his thirties or older should be able to offer some more practical evidence of achievement than paper qualifications. There are some people, including inevitably some with excellent paper qualifications, who prefer a student's life to a life of practical accomplishment. With each paper qualification acquired, they prefer to carry on a stage further as a student rather than accept adult respon-sibility. This is not to decry education or continual striving for individual educational improvement. It is merely a warning that paper qualifications are generally evidence of success as a student, not evidence of managerial or specialist achievement.

Nonetheless there may be some evidence to be gained from qualifications. In some fields involving management of professional staff, it is probably desirable that candidates have the appropriate professional qualification. This is mainly for reasons of staff morale. Remember that the qualification itself, particularly if it was acquired some years ago, is not necessarily a guarantee of either professional or managerial competence.

It is arguable that some professional exams are based on a syllabus that is twenty years behind the state of knowledge and best practice. This is a serious matter in an age of fast increasing knowledge and technique.

Many qualifications are given away on the basis of experience or some other qualification. This happens for a number of reasons. For instance the British Computer Society, operating in a relatively new field, introduced its own professional qualifications. It could not hope to persuade its existing members to take the exams. So up to a given cut-off date members were assessed, no doubt very carefully and appointed to a professional grade without an exam. The method is no doubt just as effective as an examination. Some other professional bodies also award membership on the basis of assessment of practical experience to elderly people — the over 35's for instance.

However, I know of one young man, an extremely pleasant and competent person. He worked as a clerk in the sales office of a large company. He applied for and was given a job in a 'professional' institute. As part of the arrangements for the new job, he was offered associate membership of that body.

In the government service in particular, great emphasis is placed on formal educational qualification. The higher civil service appear to have a built-in suspicion of anyone without a degree, whatever their age. I once came across an odd case in a nationalised industry. The manager of a computer centre retired on grounds of ill health. The deputy, who had his failings, but was perfectly competent to do the job and who had managed a centre before was promoted on a temporary basis. However he was relatively low on the list for promotion and eventually another man, with much less knowledge and experience of computer centre management was moved in. He happened to be higher on the list of those qualified for promotion and had had some experience in computer centre work. The fact that the acting manager was better qualified for the particular job was not allowed to sway the decision.

In operating by the rules, Buggins got promoted in his turn — the competent acting manager was required to remain as his deputy and effectively carry him till he had learnt the job. This could only happen in the public sector or conceivably in a family firm. However, more of Buggins turn later.

Assessing people for promotion or for appointment to a senior post by their paper qualifications is a lazy way of doing things. Most personnel managers would probably argue that it is used only as a preliminary requirement to sieve out the candidates. Yet it may succeed in sieving out the very man most likely to succeed in the job.

In selecting people for promotion you are not primarily concerned with rewarding them for past good work or for providing them with an automatic step up on the basis of some moss-covered qualification; you are selecting the person who will perform best in the job to be filled. In doing so you are trying to forecast his performance from such evidence as is available. This is a difficult task and not one to be lightly undertaken. Given that past performance is probably the best guide, it is of key importance that line managers take care in assessing and recording the performance of their staff each year. This provides the basis for sound internal promotions. It provides the best information on which judgements may be made.

5

When to Promote

When should people be promoted? This may seem a silly
question. After all you promote people when you need them
and that is that. It is, however, too simple a view of things.

Promotion, as well as being used to fill jobs that have to
be done, can also be an instrument of policy. It can alternatively be an automatic or near automatic matter. For
instance, army officers, once commissioned, can be sure of
promotion at set intervals up to the rank of major subject
to passing promotion exams — for which special training
in army time is normally provided — and subject to the
necessary recommendations based on performance (or
behaviour!). A small proportion fall by the wayside but
the majority of young officers are carried steadily upwards
by the escalator.

VACANCY OR REORGANISATION

The most common cause of promotion is still probably to
fill a vacancy caused by death, illness, retirement, expansion
or is consequent thereon. In large organisations the occurrence
of such a vacancy can cause a ripple of transfers and
promotions. Some organisations operate a rule that a man
must always be transferred to a different department on
promotion. This, while it has many advantages, particularly
in those organisations concerned with finance or security

43

(and which may consequently be open to corruption), can also give rise to a fiendishly complicated series of moves.

In any case, the mere fact of a vacancy occurring does not mean that it is necessary to fill it. Whenever a vacancy occurs, the first automatic reaction should be to evaluate the need for the job to be done at all. Can the work be split up among the manager's colleagues or subordinates? Can some minor reorganisation combined with a redistribution of work make it unnecessary to fill the job? The mere automatic filling of every staff or managerial job by promotion or transfer is one of the reasons for low average productivity at such levels.

In many organisations, personalities play a great part in the working of the organisation. Desirable changes are put off because they would not be acceptable to Mr A or because of demarcation disputes between Mr B and Miss C. Whenever a vacancy occurs in such organisations, there should always be a pause before promoting to fill the job. Does the vacancy give the added flexibility needed to effect a change which has been held up for personality reasons? This job need not be directly involved but a transfer into it may permit reorganisation elsewhere.

Nobody, at any level in an organisation, should be allowed to believe that he will automatically succeed either to a particular vacancy or to the next vacancy to arise. It can lead to complacency. If, in the event, someone else is promoted into the vacancy, it leads to a great deal of damaging ill feeling.

TO RETAIN OR REWARD?

Should promotion be used as a bribe to keep someone in an organisation? Sometimes a key man in an organisation becomes restive and is on the point of being tempted away. In such circumstances it sometimes seems that promotion is the only thing that will keep him. Yet his value to the organisation lies in his continuing to do his present job, for which he is eminently well suited.

The problem may be that he is getting stale and feels the need for a change of surroundings. If this is the case it will soon start to show in his performance, if it hasn't already.

Promotion of itself is no solution to this problem. Dispatch on a trip to advise on an overseas subsidiary or to present a paper at some professional jamboree may be more likely to improve the situation.

The problem may, however, be one of money or status. Many real experts seek promotion from being users of a particular expertise to becoming administrators or managers purely so that they can obtain more pay. Similarly managers, particularly in the private sector, become obsessed with their money rewards and feel it necessary to obtain a steady increase in real money rewards. If an organisation will benefit from keeping the manager or specialist in his present job then they should simply pay him more — as much as he is worth or enough to keep him, whichever is the less. It is foolish to allow rigid pay rules to force you into losing a man or promoting him into a job in which he is of less value to you. It may be that this requires a formal upgrading of his job and consequent promotion for him. The grading of jobs should not be set in concrete for ever. If a man is ideally suited for a job, then the grading of that job should be pushed up despite the bleats of personnel officers beavering away to maintain neat rational organisation charts. When this man finally leaves the job, it can always be re-rated. In the case of the real top notcher, it will in any case probably have to be split between two or more people unless another top notch performer can be found.

The real problem may be status rather than money. British society — and many others — is very concerned about status. A particularly disturbing element is the non-working wife, who tends to develop a memsahib complex. For her, it is not sufficient that her husband brings in enough money for his family and enjoys his job. She feels her standing in the community depends upon his progress. She feels the need for him to have the title manager and in due course, director. This tends to be more of a problem in provincial towns or in towns where employment is dominated by a single organisation. It is quite easy to solve with apparent promotions. As long as a man is given a new title and everyone is told that he has been promoted, this is frequently sufficient. A company can ring the changes between Manager, Director, Executive,

Consultant or even Adviser. Various prefixes can be used, e.g. section, department, division, sector, segment or group manager. A title can be allowed to go out of use and then be reintroduced at a higher status level.

This all seems very trivial and in an ideal world could be treated with contempt. Unfortunately we do not live in an ideal world. A high proportion of people in hierarchical organisations lack any inner faith in themselves. They are insecure and need the props of external support, provided by titles and other signs of status. Appearances are often more important to people than realities. No doubt the climate will change in time, but until it does the use of 'apparent' promotion can be an effective weapon in retaining people of value to an organisation.

Can promotion be used in the same way to reward people for a job well done? On the whole, people should be promoted in anticipation of what they will do in the new job rather than as a reward for having completed an awkward or difficult task. If on the upward path, a man may expect promotion to follow as a reward for achievement and this is quite normal and proper — provided, that is, that he is believed to be capable of dealing with a bigger job. Most people reach a point where they are content to ease off. They would rather live comfortably than face change. To promote people in these circumstances can be a mistake. It is in effect following the Peter Principle and promoting them to their level of incompetence. Perhaps more accurately it is promoting them beyond their motivation. It may even remove their last spur to performance. It is perhaps the characteristic that strikes the outsider most about the Civil Service, that people once promoted as a reward for long service and good conduct have security of tenure. Profit-making organisations can not afford to promote merely as a reward.

TO DISPOSE OF MISFITS

It used to be said that the way to get rid of MPs who had served their purpose but who had safe seats, was to 'kick them upstairs'. They were given a peerage. In other words,

The weight of passengers can become enough to sink the ship

they were promoted from the operational part of Parliament to the House of Lords. They could sleep in peace with enhanced prestige while a more effective man could be elected to their seat in the Commons.

A similar technique is sometimes employed in the top echelons of large organisations. A man has given his whole working life or a large part of it to an organisation. He has made a major contribution to its success. Yet he has reached a point where he is now a hindrance rather than a help. His judgement can no longer be relied on. He makes mistakes. He acts as a brake on the organisation or an important part of it. Yet he can not tear himself away from the organisation. It is his life. Something must be done. He will eventually ruin or stagnate the organisation. But there is a large fund of loyalty to him for past performance and he has great influence outside the firm. The answer may be to promote him or kick him upstairs. The Chief Executive can be made President. Managing Directors can be made Deputy

47

Chairmen with special responsibility . . . . Working Directors can be moved to a 'without portfolio' directorship with special responsibility for advising on . . . . The Sales Manager can be made Chairman of a Users' Liaison Group. Special part-time consultancy posts can be created. However no organisation can afford to do this on too generous a scale. At any one time there may be one or two figureheads who can be carried in this way. The cost may well be covered by the additional goodwill generated. A spare wheel at the top can do a lot to develop good relations with the public, with customers and with those who influence graduates and school leavers in their choice of jobs.

If, however, an organisation is over-generous and every senior misfit or manager who is past it becomes a consultant, then the weight of passengers can become enough to sink the ship.

TIMING

Timing is an important aspect of promotion. Indeed, timing is implicit in everything said in this chapter. In some organisations — for instance in the armed forces — promotion for junior officers is effectively independent of establishment. If a man has qualified by passing his exams, by recommendations and by time served, he is promoted irrespective of whether or not an appropriate vacancy is available at the moment of promotion. This is important to him because both his pay and status are tied to the promotion. As an aside, this tying of pay and status to promotion has inevitably led to a devaluation of rank. In the nineteenth century a Royal Engineers Lieutenant probably did many jobs and carried responsibilities that would now require the rank of Colonel. In his day, the Lieutenant RE had just as much respect and acted as resourcefully and competently as his modern counterpart of more exalted rank. The armed services can afford to promote in this way because, at least in the past, their role implied the need for some reserve of talent in peacetime, which was available to carry the increased load in wartime. It could be argued that this justification no longer exists because the emphasis on more thorough training in peacetime plus the change in peacetime role from colonial garrison to European defence force plus internal security of the UK removes the need for such active over-manning. However, be that as it may, most organisations can not afford to promote before a vacancy exists. Some larger organisations, mostly in the public sector, keep a short list of those ready for promotion to the next grade. When a vacancy occurs, they merely promote the man at the top of the appropriate list. This requires an assumption that a man of a given grade can be promoted into any one of a variety of jobs one grade up. This may be true enough in the clerical type jobs done by the executive grades of the Civil Service, but is less likely to be true in more flexible commercial or industrial environments.

On the face of it we are driven back to timing promotions to coincide with the occurence of vacancies. Yet there is a case for trying to concentrate the bulk of promotions and consequent transfers into one particular period. You can not of course cover promotions necessary because of death or accident in this way.

One way of timing promotions is to relate them to the organisation's financial year. Many organisations try to start each financial year with an organisation that will last without major change until the end of the year. Each manager starts the year with a freshly agreed budget, allocation of resources and objectives or targets. This is the ideal time to make the bulk of promotions.

Each newly promoted manager starts with a relatively clean slate and has a full year in which to achieve his targets. There are some difficulties. The newly promoted manager is faced with an organisation, objectives and budget, which he will find difficult to alter during the year. However, it does mean that by the time he comes to prepare the following year's budget estimates he will have a reasonable idea of the problems and opportunities facing him.

A problem in this annual promotion period is that many of the promotions will be necessitated by retirements. The people concerned may not be due to retire for several months. This can give the new manager a generous run-in period with the old manager there to guide and advise him. This may prove a mixed blessing. In most cases, a handover period of a couple of weeks is adequate and a longer period is an embarrassment.

What then can be done with the old managers in their remaining months? They can be retired early, though this may have some pension scheme complications. They can be gradually wound down, i.e. given shorter working weeks and longer holidays. Ideally they should in any case be moved away from their old department or division within two or three weeks. They can still be employed gainfully in the remaining few months. The work they are given should make use of their accumulated knowledge and experience in a non-executive capacity. The ways of doing this are many. They can write training or user manuals. They can be used to inspect and report on branch activities and performance. They can prepare reports evaluating existing or future problems and opportunities, or can be employed on recruiting drives or indeed on a wide range of existing assignments.

It is popularly believed that people about to leave an organisation can not be relied on to do a thorough or competent job. This however is frequently not so when someone is about to retire finally. If he is given a clearly defined short-term job, he more than likely wants to do a good job and be seen to do a good job so that he finally leaves with a good feeling.

There may be times when an organisation has identified the person they want to promote to fill a new job that they intend to create or make vacant at some time in the future. If the man is becoming restive, it may be necessary to make some move to keep him happy in the organisation until the right time comes. This might be done by letting him in on the secret and promising him the job and the promotion that will go with it. There are, however, dangers about making promises about future plans. After all 'The best laid schemes o' mice and men gang aft agley'. Circumstances may change, a better candidate may turn up. Worse still the organisation may need him to do a job which, though of critical importance to the organisation, is less attractive to him. The best solution probably to give him a special project which keeps him too busy to think about his problems for a while. If this is accompanied by a financial inducement, he can be kept 'warm' without disclosing to him his next move. As in many other fields, it is wise for an organisation to keep its options open as long as practicable.

6

Selection Methods

In small organisations, promotion may be a fairly haphazard business, but as they become larger and particularly as they become run by managers rather than owners, the need for specific selection methods becomes pressing. It is not sufficient to have a generalised promotion policy; there must also be some rules governing the mechanics of the process of selection.

Promotion is a very emotive business. For any organisation to function reasonably efficiently and happily it is necessary for those who are not promoted to recognise that the process of selection has been fair. For this to be achieved, it is a great help to use methods that are consistent and known to everyone in the organisation who wants to know about them.

BUGGINS' TURN

This slightly perjurative term is used to describe a selection method common in bureaucratic organisations and colonial style administrations. In effect the organisation has a pool from which people are promoted in turn on the basis of seniority or length of service. The system can be seen at work in a modified form in some private companies. It is usually to be found in those organisations which are slow to change. It may be found in well established monopolies and some family-controlled firms may use it for non-family members. This fits in with the ethos of rewarding long and faithful service, which is common in some family-controlled firms.

Where 'Buggins' turn' is in operation, much time is devoted to calculating one's chances and those of one's contempories and seniors. Every time someone disappears from the system by leaving prematurely for misconduct, days of working time are misused as everyone calculates the effect on the promotion stakes. Each person can predict his future progress pretty accurately.

The emphasis is on avoiding misconduct or rather avoiding discovery. It is essential to keep your 'nose clean'. This tends to breed an atmosphere of caution. In such organisations you are not blamed for failing to take opportunities but you may be heavily blamed for making mistakes. This results in turn in an unwillingness to make decisions, a keenness to refer any problem upwards or sideways rather than risk making a wrong decision.

The system does eliminate a lot of individual competition and, within its limitations, is fair. It probably works satisfactorily in a purely administrative setting such as a colonial administration. It is totally unsuited for productive industry or commerce.

In some cases it is modified by the need to pass exams and obtain a requisite number of recommendations from one's superiors. While this may make it acceptable for the Civil Service or armed services, the vices of the system remain and a major problem of such organisations is how to allow fresh air into the upper reaches.

NOMINATION OR APPLICATION?

Should people be nominated for promotion by their superiors or by the personnel department? Alternatively, should every vacancy be openly declared and competed for by any who care to apply for the job? Nomination keeps the whole matter of promotion firmly in the hands of the relevant management. They select the field of candidates to be considered as well as making the final selection. Under such a system, people may feel that they are being kept down by their own management. Perhaps they feel they are not being given a chance because they have become indispensible in their present job.

A system of announcing all jobs and allowing people in the organisation to apply for transfer or promotion to the job can reduce any such feeling of direct victimisation. It can also, sometimes, allow the determined and capable person, whose potential has been overlooked by his own manager, a chance. Even if he does not get the first job he applies for, it draws his manager's attention to the fact that he is keen to advance in the hierarchy. It will result in his manager watching his progress more closely in the future and he may also be given more opportunities in his existing job.

It is argued that a system of application favours the 'big-head', the ambitious pusher; it may penalise the more modest but equally or more capable person. There is something in this but the good manager can still directly encourage such people to apply for promotion to jobs for which they seem particularly well suited.

Other problems may be the volume of applications and the man whose ambitions are greater than his capabilities. The field can be kept down by the way in which the requirements of the job are defined. The requirement can be expressed both in terms of formal qualifications and length of experience of specific kinds relevant to the job. If this description is too restrictive, it may be rumoured by the disaffected that the job description has been specifically written around Mr A, to ensure that he gets the job.

An advantage of the system is that the person who is not really very keen on promotion need not apply for it. He may be regarded as a bit of a stick-in-the-mud by his colleagues but he does not lose face by being seen not to be selected. After all, he did not want the job and didn't apply. However, an application system may help to stimulate some movement across internal boundaries in an organisation. To the extent that it leads to people being considered and promoted across boundaries more frequently than would otherwise be the case, this is a clear benefit.

In practice many companies and other organisations operate an application system for the bulk of promotions. They are not compelled to fill the job from those who applied, though in most cases they do. If the standard is not good enough, they can readvertise, recruit from outside or even nominate someone for the job. While jobs in the lower and middle range may be filled in this way, there appears to be less keenness to fill more senior posts like this. In particular, top jobs in any organisation seem rarely to be filled by open application and competition. There are too many political overtones affecting the organisation. The requirements of induction and preparation may also mean that a man is effectively selected months or even years before any formal announcement to him or to anyone else.

Some firms go through the motions of advertising all vacancies and accepting bids for them, but have no formal enforceable method of procedure thereafter. The applications may or may not throw up some likely candidates for consideration. In practice, the responsible manager fills the job as he wants. If he chooses, arbitrarily, to look outside for a candidate he does so. It probably needs fairly strong central control and possibly a strong trade union influence for the system to work completely fairly and openly.

In some ways an application system is expensive. It is an absolute pre-requisite of such systems that each job is adequately advertised internally in every department. Every application must be considered and acknowledged. A formal short-list must be prepared and considered.

INTERVIEWING PROCEDURES

In many fields the final selection procedure involved in promoting a person to a new appointment is an interview. This may be for promotion to a specific appointment, e.g. teachers applying for a headship or deputy headship. In others it may be selection for inclusion on a list of those suitable for promotion as with police promotion boards. In the public sector promotion boards and interviews appear to be more formal than in private sector companies. The degree of centralisation and the width of the field has some bearing on the subject. In private industry great weight is probably given to annual review procedures, to actual achievement and to the reports of managers under whom possible candidates have worked. At senior levels much of the 'interviewing' will have been done quite informally and unannounced in advance of any formal consideration. At lower levels, there may be formal interviews by the manager responsible, possibly assisted by a personnel officer. These range from an informal chat to see whether the manager likes the colour of the candidates eyes to a properly conducted interview.

In many organisations a more formal interview board is held, at which a number of people interview the candidates. I remember sitting as a member of such a board to select the deputy head teacher of an infants school and I think that experience well indicates many of the drawbacks of the system. The candidates appeared in turn to sit at a table, at which nine people sat to interview them. The nine were the chairman of the education authority and six other members of the board, drawn from members of the council of the local authority and members of the schools governing body. The remaining two were the head teacher and an educational adviser from the education department.

We were provided with a duplicate sheet about each candidate. This gave the usual personal and professional history together with two or three short paragraphs listing 'main points from letter of application'. Each one brought out some meritorious point about interest in voluntary work or some special aspect of infant education. There was no formal report of how they had actually performed in their existing or previous posts. We were also provided with a list of suggested questions in case we were not bright enough to think up any of our own.

In a little preliminary discussion it was suggested we should ask one question each. The nicely dressed and very presentable education adviser has stuck in my memory ever since as the person who spoke of a 'new innovation', a solecism that might be expected from poorly educated managers like myself but seemed inappropriate from a professional educational administrator speaking in that capacity.

From the sheets of details, the candidates were fairly well balanced. Two of the candidates were teaching at the school to which the appointment was to be made and hence the head teacher was able to comment on their performance. One candidate seemed slightly over-qualified in that she had an honours degree.

The three candidates appeared before us in turn showing various degrees of self-confidence or nervousness. The chairman then went round the table giving each of us our turn to ask our questions, which the candidate answered. Inevitably, because the object of the board was to compare the suitability of each candidate against the others, it was necessary to ask more or less the same question to each candidate. One member of the board asked a clever and very sensible question. 'You go past a classroom in which a student teacher is taking a lesson. You hear a burst of laughter from the classroom. What do you do?' The answers gave a very revealing view of attitudes to education. However, it was clear from the subsequent conversation, when we were considering our verdict, that this man sat regularly on boards for local head teachers and deputy heads. It was also clear that this was 'his question' which he always asked. In other words, any local teacher who did her homework could have come prepared for this question and given an answer which would have put her well up in the ratings. It was also clear from the discussion that one of the councillors had strong personal feelings about one of the local candidates. In practice, her comments were so unwisely and strongly expressed that I think she, if anything, strengthened that candidate's chances. However, it did illustrate the dangers of selection procedures for public appointments, where local politicians do the selecting.

In the end it seemed to me that the final selection process depended overwhelmingly on interview performance. Most of the questions were predictable ones concerned with the duties of deputy head, her relationship to the head, other teachers and parents, the aims of infant education and modern methods of teaching. It was the sort of board that you could be coached to do well at. An intelligent person, who took the trouble to talk to people, who had attended similar local boards, could have prepared herself in such a way as to show up well at the board. This ability to show up well at the board interview need not have any direct bearing on the ability to be a deputy head teacher.

I have written at some length on this simple case, because it may be sufficiently removed from normal commercial and industrial experience for the points to come home. In the last analysis, an interview tells you whether a candidate is good at being interviewed or not. This may be a crude generalisation but it contains more than a grain of truth.

When interview boards are an essential part of the promotion process, they should be kept as small as possible. Three members are almost certainly sufficient — a line manager, a specialist/professional if appropriate and a personnel manager. The very most there should be is five. I have sat on both sides of large selection boards. As a selector one appreciates that too many irrelevant factors enter into the selection. The interaction between board members can sway decisions. Because so many people are involved the interview tends to be conducted at a very superficial level. Proper coaching in interview techniques, particularly for promotions at junior and middle levels, may well be more important than the qualities required in the job to be filled.

At the receiving end, it is a daunting business facing nearly a dozen people, most of whom are unknown to you. You know that your immediate chance of progress lies in their hands. You have probably been kept waiting in an anteroom, possibly with some of the other candidates. In such circumstances, I embark on such an interview in a highly nervous condition. The more important the interview, the worse I am. I do not believe that a large board can hope to be completely fair to candidates. Worse still, from the management viewpoint, it may make the wrong selections, saddling the organisation with presentable and superficial people while the able but less assured seek elsewhere.

Some organisations try to overcome the deficiencies of normal interviews by using extended selection interviews. These are expensive to run and can not generally be used for every promotion. They can, however, be used to select for promotion to one or two key levels. The extended interview is derived from the armed services officer selection boards. Some firms do not use them directly for promotion purposes, but use them for selecting or recruiting people into their fast stream (of which more in the next chapter).

In extended interviews the candidates assemble as a group for about three days. They live together with the selectors who observe their behaviour and performance during the whole of the period. The group take part in a number of discussions and contrived situations. They may go through a number of tests. This enables the selectors to obtain a far better idea of the candidates and their activities than any normal interview. It does however require the time of several relatively senior managers in order to be effective. There is also a danger that too much emphasis may be given to the selectors' personal prejudices and such irrelevancies as how a candidate eats his peas.

TESTS

Because of the shortcomings of all interview procedures, many organisations seek to find some objective way of selecting people for promotion. Surely there must be some test, or combination of tests, that will enable one to pick the winners. Such a hope seems as doomed to failure as the punter's infallible systems for picking the Derby winner.

Batteries of tests can be used to determine whether the candidate has the required intelligence and aptitudes — if the requirements can be accurately identified. Again such procedures are expensive and can be applied perhaps at one or two points on the ladder. It is argued by some people that intelligence tests are an unnecessary expense. First because educational attainment gives a broad measure of intelligence. Secondly, pure intelligence is not a key management characteristic!

Another form of test appropriate to the very large organisation is some form of promotion exam. The armed forces and the police use exams as part of the process for qualifying for promotion at the lower levels. Promotion exams can demonstrate that a certain level of background knowledge has been attained. They can demonstrate that a candidate can deal — on paper — with the sort of situation he may have to cope with at the next higher level. In a way promotion exams are merely indicators that certain standards have been attained in the course of progressive training.

In some ways the various levels of professional qualification provide the same basic indication in commercial and industrial organisations. However most management jobs are unlikely to be filled by any form of promotion exam. Its main merit is that it eliminates partisanship in part of the selection process. Hence it is a tool for ensuring that a certain level of knowledge and (on paper) competence is achieved. It is thus highly suitable for the public service, where it acts as some protection against corruption in the promotion process. My comments about competence 'on paper' apply more to service situations. Modern managers have to do a lot of work on paper and the ability to do so is certainly an essential characteristic. However, even in the modern bumph world, managers must be able to deal with people face to face and must have some understanding of practical motivation.

Although promotion exams have been largely confined to the public service in the past, we may well see them spread into large industrial and commercial organisations. The need to be seen to be fair and the need for objective tests may well be felt more strongly with the spread of state ownership and influence.

In the end, the test of whether a man should be promoted into a new job is whether he is likely to do the job well and better than any of the other possible candidates. I believe the most important indicator is still his past achievements. However, the achievements must be relevant. An experienced salesman may meet his target with 100 per cent margin three years running and still make a complete hash of the job of sales manager. Better achievement indicators would be how he had dealt with trainee salesmen put under his wing or how he had performed as a temporary manager when a sales manager was absent sick or on holiday. Such situations may have to be contrived for potential managers well before the possibility of promotion arises. As in so much else, a successful promotion policy requires foresight.

7

A Fast Stream

Selecting people for promotion is a difficult and time-consuming business. Firms recruit their professional specialists, e.g. solicitors and accountants, from among the professionally qualified. Alternatively they provide special training arrangements for people specifically recruited for the purpose into the appropriate professional department.

What is to be done about the more basic requirement for managers at all levels? Do you assume that everyone joins the firm at shop-floor level and that merit combined with effective selection methods will ensure an adequate supply of candidates for promotion through the ranks and eventually into the top jobs? This may have been a valid assumption in the days of inadequate and unequal educational opportunity. It may also have been valid in the day of small firms. In the modern industrial world the majority of people work in large organisations. In Britain people enter employment at ages from 16 to 25 or more with educational qualifications ranging from nil to a higher degree. All men may be born equal but they are no longer equal in talents, qualifications and character by the time they first enter paid employment.

Is there a need to make special provision for the recruitment of a special group of potential top managers, who can move through the lower ranks of an organisation at speed? Indeed, should they miss the lowest rungs of the ladder altogether? Should all organisations — or even some — have their preselected heaven-born ones; their officer class; their pre-Fulton administrative class of the home civil service.

A GRADUATE ENTRY

It is argued that any child with the ability can nowadays go to University and graduate irrespective of its home background and the financial circumstances of its parents. Youthful deprivation no longer breeds large numbers of late developers. The senior managers of the future are likely to be increasingly those who have had higher education, and will be predominantly graduates.

If this is true it is important for organisations to recruit sufficient graduates, who have the other necessary qualities, to provide a large enough promotion pool to feed the upper reaches of the organisation. Graduates, in turn, expect their pay and prospects to reflect the time and effort they have put in to obtaining their qualifications. If a firm recruits to fill ground-level posts in the factory, in development or in the sales force, will they get the best graduates? If they do, will the graduates stay?

Most of the graduates who will make useful managers are ambitious. By that I do not mean that they are necessarily ambitious for personal progress in terms of standing, status and pay. They are, however, certainly ambitious to do work that satisfies them. For some this means work that they can regard as socially useful. For others, it is work that enables them to put into practice the ideas and theories they have developed at university or polytechnic. For yet others, it is any real work that stretches their capabilities.

The prospect of starting, literally at the bottom of an organisation, even with assurances of preferred progress upwards, is not always attractive. For instance, one reason that British provincial police forces are able to recruit so few graduates is no doubt that the graduate has to spend his initial two years 'on the beat'. In practice, the amount of time they actually spend on the beat is normally much less because of the incidence of training. Nonetheless the image of the job and the prospect, however falsely imagined, of two years of pavement bashing inhibits the recruitment of graduates. This must have some impact on the size and quality of the pool from which senior police officers can be promoted.

NEED FOR YOUNG MANAGERS

The prime argument for a fast stream is the need for people to enter management jobs while they are still young. Youth is of course comparative but managers who are not afraid of change are needed at all levels. They need to be capable of living with uncertainty and dealing with it. If the road of promotion is too long and weighted too heavily in favour of a 'clean record', young managers will not obtain sufficient experience through making mistakes.

In practice, few organisations give their junior managers a great deal of scope. They have to operate tight constraints of policy and budget. They are judged on their achievement of agreed objectives. This is fine in terms of meeting short-term corporate objectives. It is necessary in the short term in order to make profits. But, does it produce those capable of dealing with the uncertainties that face every organisation? Does it prepare people to take responsibility?

The answer in many cases is 'No'. In most large organisations, junior managers can slip easily into becoming bureaucrats or administrators. Most situations are covered by the rules or by precedent. If they have enough common-sense to apply the correct rule or precedent and can interpret it correctly, they will get by. If they get really stuck, they can always pass the buck sideways or upwards as long as they don't do it too often.

The habits people acquire in the early years of their life tend to stay with them. If they gradually secured promotion to top levels by being a cautious, but efficient within the rules, administrator, they are unlikely to change their ways as they enter the top echelons. It seems to me essential that

Many people's attitude to work changes after the birth of their first child

junior managers get some real responsibility early and get some experience of making mistakes. It is also essential that top managers reach senior positions before they become too set and cautious in their ways. If they have to be spotted among the normal ground level entry, promoted through each level in the organisation and given the standard amount of experience at each level, they will be better qualified for old-age pension than for top management by the time they get there.

One solution might be to keep organisations small, though this can produce promotion problems, quite apart from the more obvious drawbacks. A preferred solution is to have a 'fast stream'. These people are specifically recruited as potential managers. They may then be handled in a number of different ways. The common factor is that they are trained for promotion, obtain quicker promotion than ordinary entrants to the organisation and provide a pool from which the top managers are eventually promoted.

Most such schemes make some provisions for people who join the organisation by normal entry to move across to the fast stream. This is intended to provide a safety valve and also to provide for late developers. Many people's attitudes to work, to learning and to responsibility change rapidly after marriage or the birth of their first child. Economic realities sometimes concentrate the mind at this time and may result in a man putting forth his whole effort to improve his position at such a time. In the long run such a man may well prove better value than those who have moved effortlessly through.

Despite all the improvements in educational opportunity there may still be some who, for reasons of family background or other circumstances, may not do well in the conventional education system and only develop after some experience as an adult in the adult world. Any fast-stream system must make provision for such people. If it doesn't the organisation may lose them. However, this is probably the least of the adverse possibilities. They may lack the will or confidence to make a move and instead become a focus for discontent and dissatisfaction in the firm. It is of such stuff that revolutionaries are made — it is better to have them on your side.

EFFECTS ON RECRUITMENT

Implementing a fast stream can have a considerable impact on recruiting. First of all, it should have a direct impact in enabling you to take your pick from among the newly qualified or graduated. It is of course true that some who obtain a first-class honours degree feel that they should not be called on to make any further serious effort in their lives. However a careful selection procedure combined with a probationary period should result in an organisation being able to recruit top quality people for its fast stream.

There are however secondary effects on recruitment. People who consider applying to join an organisation give some thought to their prospects of promotion should they join. The fast stream may be seen as a block that effectively cuts off the most senior jobs from those that enter by more lowly routes. With a large fast stream — or even a well publicised one — the whole upper part of the pyramid may appear cut off. Even if the fast stream is only large enough to provide people to fill 50 per cent of the middle and senior management posts there will be a considerable impact on normal recruitment. If nearer 100 per cent of the top jobs are filled from such entrants, this effect may become very marked.

It is not just promotion prospects that affect recruitment. Fast-stream entrants clearly have to learn quite a lot before they move into the middle management jobs. A Cook's Tour of the organisation over two or three years used to be one way of handling this. This provided a form of induction training. It did not, however, prove very successful and is now largely discarded. The need is seen to provide trainees from the fast stream with real work that is both interesting and challenging. Doing so reduces the number of interesting jobs to which lowlier entrants can progress. The main effect is to choke off applicants who are not well enough qualified for the fast stream. In particular, those whose educational qualifications are not of the best but who still have a determination to make personal progress and a contribution to the group in which they work, will be discouraged from joining the organisation. These are probably the people who would make excellent supervisors and junior managers. Some of them would make good middle or even senior managers in due course. In trying to ensure a high quality fast stream, from which to draw future senior managers, you may do serious damage to the organisation by depleting the quality of the pool from which your lower layers of management should be drawn.

67

Many will argue that this is not true, that the quality of recruitment generally is enhanced by a well publicised fast stream. They may even point to the large numbers of graduates that the old UK Civil Service was able to attract into the executive class — a very definitely second-class route of entry compared with the administrative class. However a degree is not in itself evidence of determination; independence of mind and a desire to make an effective contribution. Nor is the fact that many such people find their way to the top ranks on an equal basis with the fast stream necessarily evidence. After all, in a strictly strutured hierarchy, operated to some extent on the principle of Buggins' turn, suction must pull up whatever proportion of lowly entrants is judged appropriate.

To some extent the result of dismantling the fast-stream structure appears to have results that are more cosmetic than practical. For instance, the fact that every army officer has to spend a period in the ranks before going to Sandhurst does not alter the fact that Sandhurst entrants to the army are a very large fast stream compared to the bulk of recruits. Has the abolition of the class system in the UK Civil Service really had much effect on the promotion balance?

MOTIVATION

The effects of a fast stream or favoured class of entrants does not stop at recruitment. It can permeate a whole organisation. Some youngsters do not realise the implications of a fast stream when they join. Some, particularly school leavers, may not even be aware of its existence. However, they will soon learn once they are in. As they look up the pyramid, they will see entry to the top jobs blocked off by the fast stream. They will see new fast stream entrants make mistakes in the junior posts, in which they get their training, and still move fast up through the organisation.

Of course, whether you have a fast stream or not, some people will move fast up the promotion ladder. However, a formal creation of a class structure with people in a preferred class at entry — with guaranteed better prospects — can have a severely demotivating effect on the remainder of the work force. It can give rise to widespread feelings of jealousy. I stress this not because I think fast streams are bad but because I believe the effects on the motivation of other staff must be considered most carefully. It would be totally unreasonable to expect a 16 year old school leaver with no academic qualifications to start with the same salary and prospects as a graduate of 21. Yet we must also recognise that by the time they are both 25 they may be of equal value to the organisation. This can happen if the school leaver realises his position and is determined to rectify it while the graduate has burnt himself out in obtaining his qualification and if he regards that qualification as a meal ticket for life.

Fortunately it is easier to arrange matters in a commercial or industrial organisation than it is in a more strictly structured organisation. It is perfectly possible to deliberately recruit well qualified potential high-fliers on a basis that gives them a flying start without making them part of a mandarin class. One commonly adopted method is to recruit them at a competitive market salary with a guaranteed rate of salary progress, subject to their manager's approval and recommendation. These guaranteed rates can in fact be a selection of rates according to whether the entrant is rated in practice a grade 1 performer down to a just acceptable grade 5. They are employed in real jobs. Even though they are junior jobs, they are stretched and their brains used. They are given no outward priviliges or status. The real start that they are given is that they are subject to careful scrutiny and evaluation from their first day in the organisation.

If they do well, they probably start moving into management by the age of 25. If they do not do well they do not enter the management stream. Tougher companies may sack them. Softer hearted ones may allow all but the utterly idle and incompetent to be gradually absorbed into the normal workforce in some clerical job. Very limited salary increases, particularly in times of inflation, soon place them firmly back in the 'crowd'.

This does mean that industry and commerce can hope to recruit people from among the good brains leaving university each year. They can be coached from day one so that their potential is continually developed. They can be encouraged to move up the pyramid as rapidly as possible. Providing these fast-stream entrants are not given all the middle and top managerial jobs they should enable the organisation to develop a good supply of young managers.

In some ways the critical factor in both the public and the private sector is to combine two essential requirements: first, to make the scheme attractive enough to obtain the best available entrants. Because the young you want tend to be optimistic, they can probably be recruited on the basis of good salary provided they are convinced that future opportunities really are there if they do perform.

The second essential requirement is a humane method of disposal of those who do not come up to expectations. This is a matter of being fair to the man, being fair to the other people in the organisation and not doing anything to tarnish the organisation's reputation in the eyes of future potential fast-stream recruits.

Many years ago I met a Principal in the UK Civil Service. He joined the Service as an administrative class entrant — an Assistant Principal. At the age of 60 he had moved up one grade to Principal. This promotion happened almost automatically after 2 years service. When he retired he was allowed to stay on in the department in a much lower grade doing a key clerical job. He did the job well, much better than it had been done before. He seemed very happy doing it. The concensus of opinion was that he was much better suited to the job than he had been in the comparatively responsible post of Principal where he had been a fearful delaying and frustrating factor.

People in middle seniority and top jobs need some security of tenure. They need some safeguards to enable them to act firmly and reasonably independently. They need, just as much as the mass of the workforce, some assurance of their treatment. Yet in some areas of organisational life the pendulum has swung too far in favour of security of tenure. In designing fast-stream promotion, it is essential to avoid providing fast-streamers with a guaranteed ladder and security of tenure, irrespective of performance.

8

Grooming for Promotion

Do people develop automatically? Are there born leaders and managers? If you can find these people and put their foot on the first rung of the ladder is that all that is necessary?

Many people feel when they leave school or university that their education is complete. They feel they have reached the mountain top rather than the first range of foothills. Some organisations, impersonally, seem to take a similar view. Training of any sort is regarded as a 'fill-in' rather than something of primary importance. External training is regarded as an expensive luxury. Coaching for management jobs may happen accidently, but is not pursued as a matter of policy.

THE NEED

The organisations that are most successful in developing their managers appreciate that there is a need to do something active to help the development. It will not happen automatically, though a few highly motivated people will do something to develop themselves. However this too has its dangers, as they may be motivated to migrate to an organisation that does do something positive to develop its managers. A possible way out is to recruit externally to fill middle and senior posts for which no suitable person in the organisation has been developed. If this involves too high a proportion of external recruitment, it has an adverse affect on the morale of the organisation. Another possibility is just to promote the best available men or the next most senior man and hope it works out — a very common practice.

These are very amateur approaches. Any organisation needs a positive policy to identify those who are capable of undertaking more responsibility and a policy for actively developing those who have been so identified. In fact there is a case for developing not just a chosen few but a wide spectrum of employees. There should be some scope for self-selection. The man who really wants to develop and who actively seeks greater responsibility may well be a better bet than the more passive better qualified person, identified by his manager or the personnel department as possessing potential.

Self-selection can be carried too far. In one company I know of, all junior and middle management jobs were filled on the self-selection principle. Most of these jobs were advertised internally. Potential applicants could 'phone up and discuss the job and its implications but if they wanted to apply they had to do so through their existing manager. This led to a number of games. Some people applied for jobs outside their division to encourage their own division to think more carefully about their pay and promotion. On the other hand some managers resented their people applying for jobs outside the division. If they failed to get the job, then such managers held it against them that they had been disloyal in applying to move.

Another oddity of the system in this company was that it was very fond of employing managers as project managers and in other short-term appointments lasting anything from three months to several years. Typically such appointments lasted one or two years. When the manager came to the end of his appointment, he was left to find and negotiate his own next job. Quite competent but not personally pushing managers found this quite demoralising. Some found it as easy to look outside the company as inside.

WHAT HAS TO BE DEVELOPED?

If you look down a list of management training courses and
their contents you might be led to believe that it is a matter
of learning about budgets, PERT, profit and loss statements,
interviewing, appraisal and so on. These are of course
important matters. Managers do need to acquire knowledge
of many techniques and skills. However there are more
important matters for the manager and particularly the
manager who is headed for the top or somewhere near it.
These are less tangible matters — and hence less easy to
specify for a training prospectus. A manager's judgement
has to be developed. He has to develop his power to judge
people and situations. He has to learn to discriminate
between what is vital and what is desirable. He has to learn
to cope with situations where priorities conflict and resources
are inadequate. He has to learn how to assess risks.

The manager has also to develop a number of other skills,
which are useful at most levels. His ability to understand
people must be developed. He needs to improve his communication skills, both oral and written. The manager's
knowledge and understanding of the wider context in which
he works needs to be developed. In business he needs to
understand something of how the other main departments
of his firm operate; how his firm compares with others in
the same line of business; the markets in which his firm
operates; trade union organisation and attitudes as they
affect his firm; how government departments and agencies
affect his firm.

The manager needs to develop his negotiating ability.
Every manager faces some negotiating situations, if only the
matter of his next pay rise. As he rises up the hierarchy the
more likely it is he will be involved in negotiation. Those
who grow up in sales or marketing environment may
naturally develop their negotiating skills. For those who
come up through production or engineering or who work
in a public sector bureaucracy, the need to specifically
develop negotiating skills is more pronounced.

However the most important quality that has to be
developed is self-reliance. Clearly one is not looking for the

rash willingness to 'chance one's arm' at every opportunity. Nor are we looking for people who have closed minds and refuse to consider any input from their colleagues. What we need to develop is the power to consider all the evidence, obtain whatever advice or evidence is necessary and then to make up one's mind. The manager who has to ask his senior whenever a decision is needed is a dead loss. He merely acts as a filter and delaying factor. Some people will never develop any great degree of self-reliance. When they make a decision they worry about it. In extreme cases they cannot leave their decisions alone. They modify them and reverse them like a small boy with a yo-yo. I once worked for a manager who rejoiced in the nickname of Wibbly-wobbly. I and my colleagues did not rejoice.

Self-reliance should not be confused with aggressive pushiness or a loud mouth. Determination and self-reliance are not incompatible with a modest low-key approach. Self-reliance is perhaps the quality which takes a manager through a bad patch when things go wrong. The resilience to go through a bad patch and come out fighting is most important. It may be argued that by the time adult life is entered, it is too late. A man is either self-reliant and resilient or he isn't. There are extremes where this is true. It is nonetheless possible to develop these qualities where they are latent.

DEVELOPMENT METHODS

How then are these qualities to be developed? Conventional training courses can certainly make some contribution with the more basic skills. But I believe most strongly that the more important and less mechanical management skills and attributes are best developed by coaching and learning by doing. The two, will of course, overlap. The oldest forms of training are perhaps sitting by Nellie and being thrown in at the deep end. They have over the years been denigrated by educationalists. Yet properly controlled, they do have something to offer.

There is no doubt that a good manager can provide an example from which those responsible to him can learn.

There is a lot more to coaching than that. Coaching is a matter of positive guidance. It involves explaining to the person being developed why decisions have been made, how they have been arrived at and why one decision was taken rather than the alternative. A useful method of coaching is to get the person being coached to report exactly how he has tackled a task and how he has reached the various decisions involved. The aim of coaching is to start the young manager thinking about what he is doing and why he is doing it. During the coaching process, the trainee does real work but under fairly close observation and knowing that he will be called upon to explain himself.

Not everyone can do a good job as a coach. Sympathetic understanding is required. More important, the coach must be prepared to see mistakes made without promptly jumping into the situation himself. Making mistakes, understanding why they are mistakes and how they could have been avoided is one of the best ways of learning. It is possible for an over-bearing and insensitive coach to crush a trainee with his mistakes. A good coach will make sure the trainee understands the situation; and will save the situation from going too badly wrong.

In planning the development of managers with a firm it is important to match the trainee to his seniors. Over a period each young manager should have the opportunity of working for a manager who is a good coach.

A most important part of developing managers is learning by doing. This may take the form of a carefully designed promotion in which they do the real job. This is clearly advantegeous, but suffers from one disadvantage. Specialisation has resulted in even junior management jobs in a large organisation being somewhat limited in scope. The future senior manager needs to be developed to cope with more complete situations. It may be that there are some small discrete units, perhaps an overseas branch or a self-contained subsidiary on which the future top manager can cut his teeth. A more common source of training-by-doing is projects. Most firms have a series of projects that need to be done. It may be conversion to metric standards, the absorption of another firm, the opening of a new branch, the introduction

of a new product or a re-equipment programme. These are all
suitable jobs for the trainee manager with some experience
to project-manage and to learn by doing. Some senior
managers may be aghast at allowing a trainee to play with
something of such importance and refuse to do it. People do
however respond to responsibility. It gives them a chance to
prove themselves. The good future manager will take the
opportunity and develop himself in the process.

APPRAISALS

An important method of development is the appraisal system.
It has other advantages. In particular it provides a record of
how each person in an organisation has performed against
his objectives. This can provide important evidence of
achievement when people are being considered for promotion.

Most appraisal systems are based on an annual performance
review. Each man meets his manager to discuss his performance
over the year and a synopsis of the discussion is recorded on
an appraisal interview form. The primary aim of the system is
to identify ways in which the man's performance may be
improved — both by himself and by the firm. The system is
designed to:

1   Examine systematically the way in which he has
     performed against his objectives during the period
     under review.
2   Tell the man what his manager thinks of his performance.
3   Allow the man to say how he sees his own performance.
4   Discuss the man's strengths and weaknesses.
5   Allow the man to express his ambitions and ideas on
     how his career should progress.
6   Record the manager's view on the man's future employ-
     ment.

Item six is sometimes recorded by the manager after completion of the interview and not disclosed to the man. The
appraisal interview, if carried out sympathetically and tactfully, gives an opportunity for a manager to draw attention to
ways in which performance can be improved. Weaknesses can

be discussed and suggestions made for overcoming them. As part of the appraisal an action list should be compiled. This may range from training courses to be arranged to amendment of objectives.

The appraisal interview can be an excellent opportunity for coaching an individual and gently drawing his attention to ways in which he can improve his performance. One manager of my acquaintance always holds his appraisal interviews in the morning and then takes the interviewee out to lunch. It is a nice gesture and helps to keep the atmosphere friendly. This is an important point as he takes the whole proceedings very seriously and doesn't pull punches in highlighting weaknesses and performance shortfalls.

It can be argued against the appraisal system that any serious problem or lack of performance cannot be allowed to go unchecked until the end of the year. This is of course true. But the system does allow an annual review, which might not take place without it. It forces both manager and man to think about his performance and where he is going. This must be good. If he has done well it even provides an opportunity for his manager to say an extra thank you.

TRAINING PLAN

Much training of managers is haphazard. It ranges from those large firms which effectively plan the training of their managers over virtually the whole of their working lives to those which just 'don't hold with training'.

Firms need a training plan for all their managers. In the early years it will cover planned development. A profile of the end-product manager should be visualised and the development training planned to bring the individual into line with his target profile.

Planned development should not be restricted to managers but should be applied as far as possible to the whole of a work force. If in the process someone of poor educational attainment starts to show potential, firms should consider giving such people help to bring their educational standards up and groom them for management. Many firms help such employees with their Open University fees and summer schools. The Police even run a scheme for sending experienced police officers on full-time degree courses. Such provision is not purely philanthropic. The ability to think and question existing methods of operation lies at the heart of modern management. Development of staff already on the pay roll tends to be more economical than buying in ready-trained managers of uncertain quality. We all have some potential for development. If this potential can be developed, it will be productive not just for the individual but also for his firm.

9

Parallel Promotion Paths

At one time there was only one accepted promotion path; the managerial one. Further, in assessing the standing of a manager, a great deal of weight was placed on the number of people managed. It was self-evident that the manager ultimately responsible for a thousand people was of greater importance than one responsible for a section of ten.

Even in organisations that have worked on this principle there have always been some exceptions. Due respect has been paid to the small collection of staff — people qualified to advise the enterprise in a particular field, including accountants and legal advisers. Even though respect has been paid to their views in the inner sanctums of the concern, outward respect and privilege has been paid to the modern barons, those who controlled most heads in the organisation.

This has given rise to a number of undesirable consequences. First it gives rise most noticeably to empire building. This is a strong tendency even in commercial organisations, where there are financial constraints. In the public-service sector, it is a very strong tendency. This is particularly so because, once you have established a certain establishment level, it is very difficult for others to cut it back. The public servant may have a very firm incentive to increase his establishment.

Secondly it may persuade many specialists, who are not particularly interested in management for its own sake, to move into management because it offers greater standing and rewards. Thirdly, it encourages people in an organisation to think in terms of inputs rather than results. It encourages an attitude which says in response to any call for an additional output, 'Fine, I can do it but I must have more people'.

PYRAMIDS NARROW TOO QUICKLY

In an organisational world where rewards and status depend upon position in the heirarchy, pyramids narrow far too quickly. The pyramid structure works well in military organisations, for which it was no doubt originally designed. The ratio of each level is generally 1:3 or 1:4, i.e. one regiment has four squadrons each of three troops of three sections. In addition, the army has a need for an adequate supply of 'spare wheels' to replace casualties so there are generally liberal allowances of seconds in command and staff officers with a well defined place in the hierarchy of ranks. Futhermore the career span of a service officer is relatively short. From their mid-forties on they either progress rapidly or are shuffled to one side into routine jobs peripheral to the main purpose of the organisation.

In commercial and industrial organisations the management theories about span of control generally lead to each manager controlling as many as eight subordinates. In some cases where each subordinate does an identical job, the span may be considerably greater. Even where a number of headquarters staff appointments exist, this gives a rapidly narrowing pyramid. The larger the span of control, the more sharply the pyramid will narrow. This tendency is enhanced by an equally sound management principle that one should aim to shorten the lines of communications in any organisation to the shortest practicable. It follows that the number of levels of management is few. If people left the organisation infrequently — other than on retirement — the number of opportunities for promotion would be few and far between.

PROMOTION RACE DESTRUCTIVE

This can give rise to a most destructive competitive spirit. At the very lowest level there may be sufficient people not concerned with promotion to make the first level of promotion; one that does not give rise to this competition. Thereafter the pressures can be seen to be very great. There will be strong competitive pressures on everyone in managerial jobs to perform well, both to earn promotion and to safeguard their existing job. It might be thought that this is an ideal state of affairs. What could be better than to have everyone striving to perform to the best of their abilities? Unfortunately reality does not correspond with this picture. In organisations where a really competitive promotion race develops, people's prime concern ceases to be just to do a good job to the best of their abilities. They are instead concerned to be seen to do that which is necessary to become promoted. This can be destructive of any organisation.

If the organisation operates a hire and fire policy, it can become a battle ground for survival and preferment. Managers tend to concentrate on the short term at the expense of the medium and long term. The motto in such situations is: 'The long term is made up of a series of short terms. If I don't survive the short term, there is no long term for me'. A variation on this is the manager who can see no secure future for himself and therefore squeezes the situation to provide as much benefit for himself as possible. This sometimes takes the form of caning expenses and entertainment.

If an organisation is bureaucratic, the emphasis can become one of maintaining a good record. People know that doing a good job or taking an unexpected opportunity will not bring them much credit. On the other hand if they make a mistake, it will go into their record against them for ever after. It is this which makes many public-sector organisations averse to taking risks. Promotion is based on a clean record with no recorded mistakes. It follows that those who want to be promoted don't take risks and cover their tracks if they make a mistake.

I believe that excessive emphasis on promotion, a visible hierarchy and undue competition in an organisation are destructive. The form of destructiveness can vary, but the end result is to destroy the vitality and driving force of an organisation. A conflict between the objectives of an organisation and its managers develops. No organisation can afford such a situation. They must seek a solution. This goes to the roots of its promotion policy. Such a policy must find a way to avoid a single narrow ladder leading, for the individual, only to the top or to being 'passed over'.

THE PETER PRINCIPLE – A REAL THREAT

Dr Laurence J. Peter put forward the proposition: 'In a hierarchy every employee tends to rise to his level of incompetence'. This was incorporated into his humorous book, *The Peter Principle,* which he wrote with Raymond Hull. Because the book was written in a light-hearted vein, many people think of it as a joke. The Peter Principle can however be seen to be working in many organisations. To say that every employee rises to his level of incompetence would be a great exaggeration. Yet a great many people do rise to a level in the hierarchy where they do not enjoy their job and do not do it well. They are in fact incompetent. Dr Peter correctly identified the fact that this arises because people are promoted out of a job, which they do well, into another job, which is higher up in the hierarchy. The senior job always gives more status and frequently more pay and greater security of tenure. The senior jobs are generally administrative, supervisory and managerial. The powers that be in an organisation feel compelled to offer promotion to the scientist, technician or salesman who is doing a superlative job. He in turn is tempted to accept. The temptation is strong. Family pressure to accept may be considerable. There is also a widespread feeling that it may be unwise to turn down promotion. Worse, if you don't take it that fool 'X' may get it by default. The pressures to accept are very strong not only because the pay and perks go with the senior jobs but also to a great extent because the standing in the organisation and the power to influence events goes with the management job. The scientist or technician may have little say in how money or staff are

*He may in an extreme case even be provided
with the key to the directors' lavatory*

allotted. He may see his seniors in the hierarchy fail to understand a technical problem and consequently make a nonsense
of presenting a case. Even if he does not see this happen, he
fears it will if he turns down the offer of promotion and 'X'
accepts it.

One answer to the problem is to organise pay scales so that
the specialist can be well paid — as much or more than his
manager and, indeed, in exceptional cases, more than the
higher levels of management as well. He can be given the outward trappings of office, personal office and secretary, car
and so on. If the organisation persists in perpetuating class
distinctions, he may in an extreme case even be provided with
a key to the director's lavatory.

However, the most important aspect is that the highly
competent specialist should have a significant weight in
discussions on his speciality within the organisation. His
development program should not be subject to sudden
arbitrary change by administrative edict. This is not to say
that the research scientist should be allowed his head
completely or that the development engineer should be

allowed to pour resources into a technically satisfying but high priced product for which there is no demand in the forseeable future. Nonetheless these people should be able to put forward their case within the councils of the organisation. They should be entitled to receive a reasoned argument justifying a decision that is contrary to the technical case. If this is based on factors arising from a sector or discipline with which they are not familiar they should be entitled to a patient explanation and not merely faced with an imperial ukase that 'The Director says . . .' In other words the highly competent specialist should both be allowed to get on with practising his speciality and also given the opportunity to contribute to policy affecting his speciality. He should contribute as a respected member of the management team and not as an inferior.

I believe this principle should apply in most fields, not just to research and development specialists. The top flight salesman may contribute more in that role than he would as sales manager. If a computer maintenance engineer has a flair for diagnosing faults and can identify faults in a few minutes, it would be a wicked waste of resources to put him in an office as an area manager vetting overtime claims, preparing schedules and carrying out a multitude of administrative tasks.

The conventional arguments for promoting such people in this way have been the need to safeguard the man's own prospects and also the need for specialists to be managed by people who understand the speciality and not by mere administrators. Organisational solutions have to be found and adopted to meet this need. It is particularly important now when industry, commerce and government are all developing large-scale organisations and employing large numbers of specialists or knowledge workers.

PARALLEL PROMOTION PATHS

A solution adopted already in many large organisations is that of parallel promotion paths. This system allows any specialist a satisfying career in his speciality. It allows him to continue at his speciality as long as he is capable of doing so — and as long as his speciality remains relevant.

A change in attitude to management of specialist and technical staff is needed. You would not keep a dog and bark yourself. Similarly, it is a mistake to employ a real specialist and then do his job for him. By all means let the manager agree to objectives and targets with his specialists. Thereafter let the specialist direct his own work. In effect he becomes a salaried sub-contractor. If an asbestos mining company decided to employ a doctor it would not tell him how to examine his patients or the treatment he should adopt. There needs to be a more general application of this method of working. The traditional view of a manager giving orders to his subordinates is already outdated. With specialists we need to take things a stage further. Each area of speciality should be provided with its own promotion path with graded responsibility and salary. Such specialists will then look outside their speciality to their own manager only for leadership and for agreement of objectives and budgets.

The creation of parallel promotion paths does not preclude the suitably qualified specialist from moving into the general management stream. It does mean that he is not forced into it.

Parallel promotion paths are a way of reducing the destructive pressures of a narrow promotion path and of undue emphasis on promotion rather than achievement. They are also a way of mitigating the effects of the Peter Principle.

Part Three

PLAN YOUR OWN PROMOTION

10

Know Yourself

Whenever you set out to make a plan the first step is to collect all the information that may be relevant. You need this in order to identify the nature of the problem and also to see what practical alternatives are open to you.

The first step in making the plan for your own promotion — your life career plan — is to collect the relevant information. The most relevant information is information about yourself. Some of this is straightforward factual matter of the kind you are asked to write on job application forms — age, qualifications and experience. More important, however, is real knowledge of what makes you tick. How do you react to situations? What sort of person are you? What are your strengths and weaknesses? What interests you? What will you do best?

NEVER FOOL YOURSELF

James Thurber's Walter Mitty has become a legend. Mitty, a middle-aged henpecked American, spent his life day-dreaming that he was a great man of action — a world-class surgeon, a naval commander, a daredevil pilot. There is no harm in day-dreaming or even of dreaming of yourself as a man of power and influence, providing you do not confuse imagination and reality.

Collecting information about yourself is a matter of critical self-analysis, not a private self-admiration session. Having said that, it is probably true that most English people tend to underestimate themselves and their potential. They have been brought up and educated in an atmosphere in which modesty is a highly rated virtue.

In assessing yourself try to be as objective as possible. Your self-analysis is for your own information, not for publication. There are no marks to be gained either for modesty or bombastic claims. It pays to write down your assessment. The act of writing it down will help you to keep to the point and avoid drifting away into day-dreams. It also has the advantage that you can do the job in stages. It is particularly valuable to be able to come back to your assessment after a couple of weeks and revise it.

A good planner always states the assumptions on which his plan is based. In a sense some of the conclusions you reach about what makes you tick are only tentative. You think you have assessed your strengths objectively but are not absolutely certain. You can still go ahead with your plan on these assumptions. The most important thing is to recognise that they are assumptions and you may, in due course, come to recognise that they are wrong. It helps if, instead of writing your self-assessment on scraps of paper, you write it in a notebook. I would advocate the use of a substantial notebook in which you can not only set out your self-assessment but also, in due course, your plan of action. This provides you with a permanent record of your plan and the basis on which it was made.

It is very easy to fool yourself about yourself. You can take credit for your achievements but blame your failures and inadequacies on others or on circumstances. 'I would have passed my 'O' levels if only Mum hadn't had the television on all the time.' 'I would have got a first if only I hadn't had such lousy digs and had to take vacation jobs.' The excuses are endless. If I look at my own life, I can find an excuse for every failure but that is not the object of the exercise.

'He who excuses himself, accuses himself.' There is

considerable truth in the old proverb. Our objective is to get as close to the truth as possible. One way of knowing yourself is to go back over your life and summarise what you have achieved and what you have failed to achieve. Look for the reason in each case. If there were external factors that had a bearing on your success or failure, note those as well. They may provide important guidelines when you come to make your plan.

WHAT KIND OF PERSON ARE YOU?

This is not really such a difficult question to answer. In some ways, it is comparatively easy to answer because you already know and feel the answer without much heart-searching. It is largely a matter of formally recognising the facts.

Do you like people? Are you happiest when you are with a group? Or do you prefer to spend long periods alone? Do you enjoy meeting strangers? Or do you feel nervous and uneasy about it? Do you find it easy to converse with strangers or do you just freeze up and feel a fool? Do you find it easy or difficult to communicate your ideas to other people? Do you suffer fools gladly?

Your attitudes to other people will have a considerable bearing on your promotion plan. There is little point in planning your promotion on the basis of frequent moves between companies or locations if meeting strangers turns you into a wreck. Indeed your feelings about and relationships with people have a great bearing on your job itself. If you have been in your current job for some time and made no progress, is it because of the way you interact with other people?

Do you like the same thing day after day or do you prefer a change? Do you enjoy being faced by problems that arise from such change? Do you prefer to carry on your work on a routine basis, where you have an established routine and precedent to guide you?

These again are important questions both in job choice and promotion planning. If you aspire to any promotion at all in some fields you have got to be able to face up to change and situations not covered by the rules. In even the most bureaucratic and structured jobs you must be able to cope with change if you aspire to the more senior jobs.

What do you value in life? Do you rate security very highly? Some people feel very insecure and place a very high premium on security. This desire for security and a clearly perceived promotion path through an established hierarchy leads them to such occupations as the Civil Service, where they can hope to predict their career steps twenty to thirty years ahead. You may think I exaggerate, but I assure you I don't. If security and a good pension are of great importance to you, this is perfectly legitimate. It does have a considerable bearing on your promotion plan and on the steps required to enhance your promotion plan. I am not saying that promotion is not possible for the security conscious. That would not be true. However the approach is markedly different and the pace of promotion is normally slower. The need to plan for promotion is even greater for the security conscious than it is for the man or women who is prepared to take a few risks.

Are you a person of some determination or just someone full of good intentions? A wretched tramp who was the butt of everyone's contempt in a small provincial town, was once provoked into replying 'But you never knew the man I meant to be'. However sorry one may feel for such a person, it is better to learn from his example than to follow it. Are you able to make a plan and stick to it or are you continually changing your mind or flitting from task to task like a butterfly going from flower to flower on a sunny day?

If you are like a butterfly, recognise it and, if you hope for any significant promotion, do something about it. Self-discipline is perhaps the essential key to advancement in any field. Even the great artist, who may appear to be scatterbrained and disorganised, is in fact a master of self-discipline in those things that matter to his art. In the more mundane world in which most of us work it is equally important. Fortunately self-discipline is something that most people can develop if they care enough to try.

Self-discipline does not imply that you become a soulless automaton. It does imply that you can set out a plan of action for yourself and then carry it out. It does imply a degree of self-control; the ability to control your temper

*But you never knew
the man I meant to be!*

and your appetites. There are of course degrees of self-discipline.
Even a modest degree of self-discipline can be sufficient to help
you over the early hurdles in the promotion race. Fortunately,
also, self-discipline is a cumulative thing. The more you
practise it, the more it develops.

The list of questions you can ask yourself in search of self-
knowledge seems endless. Are you physically strong or weak?
Are you naturally an optimist or pessimist? Are you a happy
person or a perpetual misery? Do you prefer working with
your mind, with people or with your hands? Do you prefer
working indoors or outside? Are you self-confident or nervous?
Do you have any phobias? What are your aspirations?

Answering these questions will help you to build up a
picture of yourself as you really are. As well as asking questions
about your own character, attitudes and achievements it is also
wise to face up to your commitments. What are they and how
do they impinge on your promotion plans? Are they such that
you are not prepared to move your home? Are you prepared
to travel in connection with your job?

STRENGTHS AND WEAKNESSES

No man is expert at everything. We all have our strengths and weaknesses. It is important to recognise them. An established principle of war is 'Reinforce success'. The same principle is recognised in the Stock Exchange adage 'Run your profits and cut your losses'.

If you hope for success in life, you should build your plans on your strengths and extend them. At the same time you must avoid having to rely on the areas where you are weak. This can be done by avoiding work, which requires you to expose your weakness, or by ensuring that you cover your weakness with someone else's strength. Another possibility is to spend time trying to overcome your weakness. If you are very weak in some key attribute you may have to do this. For instance if you hope to become a managing director, you must develop some skill with people. However, in general, time spent on developing your strengths is likely to be more productive than time spent in trying to overcome weaknesses. Most organisations promote you because of your strengths and in spite of your weaknesses providing you have shown that you are aware of them.

If your strengths and weaknesses are so important to your plans for promotion, it is clearly important to recognise them. If you do not already know them, think back over your life and try to analyse the strengths that helped you at points where you have been successful. Think not just about the big successes but also about the small ones. Think about how and why you have been successful at school, university and work. Think as well about your other interests, your hobbies and other activities. Were you a great success in running a stall at a local jumble sale? Have you the knack of taking interesting photographs? Have you any particular skill? Is there anything which most people find difficult to do and which you find extremely simple to do? Are you very observant? Are you good at mental arithmetic? Do you always win at chess? Have you a very good memory?

Try to do a really thorough hunt for your strengths. Remember that all your strengths will not be equally strong. You may be quite good at reading complicated documents, understanding and summarising them. You may at the same time be able to drive a car safely and play the violin to amateur solo standard. Not only will the strengths vary in strength, they will also vary in the extent to which you can use them to good effect in your promotion plan. Nonetheless they should, as far as possible, be identified and recorded.

Weaknesses also come in all shapes and sizes. As you identify them, consider what it is possible to do about them. You may be hopeless with figures, for example, and quite incapable of even the simplest mental arithmetic. In this case, if your job involves an appreciable amount of mental arithmetic, one possibility is to acquire an electronic calulator to overcome the difficulty. If your firm won't provide it, it may still be worth buying your own.

If you know that you feel vague and sleepy after half a pint of bitter, then you should avoid drinking at lunch time. This is quite possible, even if you and your friends always have lunch at the local pub. You can always drink tomato juice. It may cause some ribbing at first, but the joke will stale after a few days.

Many weaknesses may be much more difficult to overcome. Try to identify them clearly and also the circumstances in which they come into play or let you down. You can then explore ways in which the effect of your weak points can be kept to a minimum. While you are doing this, try to avoid the situations where your weaknesses show up.

WHAT INTERESTS YOU?

In the same way as you should build on your strengths, so you should also build on your interests. Educational and industrial psychologists recognise that we do our best work when we are interested in it. We tend to be both more productive in the time available and also able to work longer if we are interested in our work.

When we work at something that interests us, we enjoy it. We produce better work than someone who is equally capable but just not particularly interested in the work. The man who is interested in his job thinks about it and finds better ways of doing it. On the whole the man who does a job which interests him is the man who is promoted. Above all, doing work which interests you provides you with a satisfying and enjoyable life.

When we plan for our own promotion, we need to recognise what interests us, so that our plan takes account of it. If the plan we make involves a high proportion of the kind of work that interests us that is a good augury for its success.

You may say, 'Well I enjoy drinking beer in the pub with the lads. That's what interests me and I don't suppose anyone will pay me to do that; not even a brewery'. Perhaps so, but it is necessary to examine your interest and enjoyment more closely. If you analyse it, you may find that it is not drinking the beer that you enjoy, but the evening-long conversation with the lads. This may be an indicator that your promotion path may lie through sales jobs or other jobs that involve a great deal of personal contact.

Of course it is not possible for everyone to turn their hobby into a job. Not every amateur poet wants to become a technical author. Although a poet writes, his interest lies in a different direction to writing technical instruction manuals. To many people a hobby is something they turn to after a day's work to enable them to relax and enjoy themselves.

There is, of course, also the matter of comparative advantage. An employer may well pay you much more to work in an administrative capacity in an office than you could earn as a poet, stamp dealer or musician. Nonetheless the point is still valid that if you work at something that interests you — even if it is not what interests you most in life — you are likely to do better than you will in a job which bores you.

ARE YOU IN THE RIGHT JOB?

Having studied yourself, as I have suggested, you may well start to ask yourself whether you are in the right job? Perhaps your present job does not interest you. Perhaps it does not use your strengths. Perhaps it makes your weak points glaringly apparent. If this is so, your promotion plan may indicate that a change of occupation is a desirable first move.

The younger you are the easier it is to make such a change. Nonetheless a great many people, having realised that they are following the wrong occupation for them, succeed in making a change in their 40s or 50s. Although I changed my career completely at the age of 36 and intend to do so again before I reach retirement, I would advise considerable caution. Having considered the problem as carefully as you can on your own, it is well worthwhile seeking professional vocational guidance.

It is also well worth remembering that if you are employed in a large organisation, they may well be able to offer you a change of direction within the organisation. This has many advantages. If you have made a mistake, you can change back with less difficulty. You start in the new occupation with the advantage of knowing the organisation. You may be able to move over into what is in effect a retraining period without a drop in salary. A lower salary and some initial expenses may be inevitable if you change employer and start a new occupation.

KNOW YOURSELF

You can only plan your own promotion successfully if you understand yourself first. No one else is likely to have the interest to really know and understand you. Knowing yourself is the essential prerequisite to developing your full potential.

11

Know Your Company

The title of this chapter should perhaps be 'Know your employer'. Whether you are employed by central or local government, by nationalised or private industry, by a big bank or a small partnership, the principle still applies. In planning your promotion a key factor is the company or other organisation that employs you.

It is not sufficient to know the company name and the address of the place you work. This is far too superficial an approach. It is important to know the extent of the company, what subsidiaries it has, what links it has with other companies, which areas and countries it operates in, the range of its products and the types of people it employs, its financial organisation, what training facilities it offers to its employees and what its promotion policies are. Perhaps even more important you need to understand the corporate attitudes.

DOES IT MATTER WHAT SORT OF COMPANY YOU WORK FOR?

My answer is 'Yes'. Clearly, if you work for a company that employs only six people, your opportunities for promotion

within the firm are very limited unless the company embarks
on a major expansion programme. That may be a rather
superficial judgement. It may, for instance, be possible to
work as an articled clerk for a small firm of accountants.
There may be an excellent prospect of becoming a partner
and helping to develop and expand the firm. The professional
trainee in a professional firm is an exception to the general
rule that very small firms offer worse opportunities for
promotion than large or medium ones.

The extent to which your company provides training
opportunities is of key importance. If you aim for promotion
up several rungs of the ladder, you have to prepare for it. To
some extent it is of course possible to learn on the job, but
it makes life easier if you can obtain some formal training in
the company's time and at their expense. Some firms have
positive training policies and plan the training of their
employees. They tie the training closely to their appraisal
system and their promotion plans.

Many companies provide very little training for managers
and this includes some quite large companies. However,
companies that do not provide formal management training
are sometimes prepared to send people on management
courses. These range from two-day courses on individual
techniques to year-long courses at university business schools.

Some companies are also prepared to release staff for a
day a week to attend local education authority courses.
Some will pay the fees for their people to attend evening
classes or to study with the Open University.

Companies differ widely in their promotion policies. At
one extreme it may depend on whether the managing director
likes the colour of your eyes. At the other extreme are
carefully thought out formal selection procedures. Some
companies work on the principle of promoting from within
the company. Others seem unable to recognise the potential
of their own employees and frequently recruit from outside
the firm rather than promote from within. Some firms
believe in moving their employees when they promote them.
Others follow a deliberate policy of moving promotees
across functional boundaries. For instance, they may expect
a customer engineering manager in the course of his career

to spend some time in a factory job and some in a marketing post. In such companies the top posts tend to go to the man who has a wide experience across the company.

In some companies people of a certain type or with a certain type of qualification appear to fill a high proportion of senior jobs. For instance, some companies seem dominated by engineers, others by accountants. In some organisations a very high proportion of managerial jobs are filled by university graduates.

Some companies operate almost exclusively in their home country. Others have widespread overseas interests. These may vary in their staffing of overseas subsidiaries or divisions. Some, as a matter of policy, fill jobs with nationals of the country in which the subsidiary operates. Others try to operate a truly multi-national policy, under which managers of any nationality are appointed to any post. Thus many head-office posts are filled by overseas managers. Some companies fill the management positions in overseas subsidiaries with people from their home base. Policies vary on how these people are treated when they return home. In some companies they are considered better qualified by reason of their over-seas experience. In others they appear to be written off — prematurely retired or fitted into non-jobs on their return home.

Some companies are organised on a centralised basis with large head offices. Recruitment and promotion policies are closely controlled from head office. Other large companies are organised on a decentralised basis with much of the power to hire, fire and promote being delegated to divisions.

All these aspects of the company you work for will have a bearing on your promotion plan. In some cases an under-standing of how your company works and is organised may convince you that you will have to move to another company to achieve your promotion aspirations. Indeed, for a young man or woman, a promotion plan may involve the planned move between several companies of different characteristics.

If your plan is going to be based on working for a company, it is also important to be reasonably certain that it will stay in business. You need therefore to understand as much as possible about the company you work for — its products, its markets and above all its financial state.

To do this you should try to read the company's own sales and technical brochures. You should also watch for comment in the serious press, particularly the *Financial Times*, *The Times*, *Guardian*, *Daily Telegraph* and *The Economist*. To find out how others see your firm's products or services, watch the technical press.

The most important source of information about your company, if it is a public company, is its annual report and accounts. A study of this document tells you a lot about a company, its financial strength and chances of survival. Some companies make copies of the annual report available to their staffs. If yours does not, your bank manager can probably get a copy for you if you ask him.

If you intend to stay with a company for any length of time, I believe it is worth buying some of its shares. Before you laugh too much, I assure you that it is possible to buy a very small number of shares in a company quoted on the Stock Exchange, quite easily. I bought 10 shares in the company that employed me in 1969 at a price of £1.77½ a share. The total cost was less than £20. Your bank manager will handle the transaction for you. I do not suggest that you invest your life savings in the company that employs you. That might be a very bad policy. What I do suggest is that anyone who really plans to get ahead can save a few pounds to buy a token holding in the company that employs him. This will ensure that he gets a copy of the annual report and accounts.

Of course, if you are employed by a private unquoted company, it will not be possible to buy shares in it. If you are employed in local or central government or a nationalised industry, the question will not arise. It is worth noting that most government organisations produce reports of some sort which can provide you with useful information. If, for instance, your work in a police force, the Chief Constable has to make an annual report to his Police Authority. You should be able to obtain a copy if you try and you will find it full of useful facts and figures. If you are employed in a nationalised industry you can probably get hold of a copy of the annual report internally or possibly from a good reference library. Failing that you can probably buy a copy from a government book-shop.

Knowing the financial state of your employer is of greatest importance in the private sector. If your company goes out of business, this can mean a serious hitch in the progress of your promotion plan. If it is taken over or merged into another company, this can result in a managerial bloodbath and will almost certainly have a direct effect on future promotion prospects. Even a move by worried shareholders to appoint a new and more dynamic chairman can materially alter the promotion prospects within a company.

If you plan to achieve promotion within a company, you must get to know that company as well as you can. Some promotion may come if you just keep your head down and do your job. You are much more likely to be promoted and consistently promoted up the ladder if you really understand the environment in which you are working. The main component of this environment is the company that you work for.

BUREAUCRACY, ENTERPRISE OR FAMILY FIRM?

In trying to understand the firm you work for it is important to appreciate that the whole spirit and style of a company can have a major impact on your promotion prospects and on how you plan to achieve promotion. As a crude generalisation you can divide companies into bureaucracies, enterprises and family firms. I have worked for firms in all three categories.

The characteristics of the bureaucratic firm make it similar in many respects to a central government department or nationalised industry. It has a formal well established organisation, which is rarely changed. When it is changed, the change is usually marginal. Considerable stress is laid on loyalty and long service. Age and experience are important. Consequently middle and top management tends to be middle aged to elderly. Status and status symbols play a large part in the bureaucratic firm. Office sizes, carpets and furniture are graded according to rank much as they are in the Civil Service. A key to the private lavatory is an important status symbol.

The feeding facilities are carefully graded sometimes into as many as seven different levels from the Works Canteen to the Directors' Dining Room. The word 'mess' is often applied to the various managers dining rooms, e.g. The Senior Managers' Mess. I can only assume that the term came into use after the First World War. Other firms may denote the level of the dining facility by a name such as 'The Blue Room'. You have to belong to the firm to know what the right to eat in the blue room signifies.

Managers expect to be treated with respect. If they enter your office you stand up — don't worry though — they usually send for you rather than visit you. If they are a couple of levels senior to you in the hierarchy they probably expect you to address them as 'Sir'.

If you hope to get on in such firms, it is helpful to have been to a public or good grammar school. A good war record or national service commission also helps. It is noticed if you play rugger or golf. Any sporting achievements tend to be plus points.

Bureaucratic firms tend to be suspicious of new ideas and are often very labour-intensive. Such firms often operate in industries serving highly controlled markets. However, many of the traditional bureaucratic firms are being forced to change their ways. This is often because of the need to compete to retain and extend markets, combined with the need to increase productivity and a changing social background.

Very recently I visited a bureaucratic organisation employing about 2500 people. I talked to their Chief Systems Analyst about how they decided what work to put on the computer and what sort of justification he had to make. He replied, 'Well, of course I do try to make a cost justification, but the truth of the matter is that if the boss likes the idea we do it, if he doesn't we don't do it however good the cost/benefit justification.'

A more modern version of the bureaucratic company exists. This is normally a large company with tens of thousands of employees. Like its traditional counterpart it is formally organised and places considerable importance on long service. But it also puts a heavy emphasis on paper qualifications. In some ways they are even more stratified than the traditional

If the boss likes the idea, we do it

bureaucratic firm. But some more senior posts are held by comparatively young men — provided they have the right qualifications. Such firms have very formal selection, annual appraisal and promotion procedures. They tend to recruit a significant number of university graduates and to groom them to fill a high proportion of the managerial ranks. They are more open to new ideas than the traditional company and tend to be more market-oriented. Accountants and personnel managers play an important part in such companies. However, these companies are still relatively slow to change. Committees play an important part in their running.

The enterprise is an entirely different kind of company. It is results-oriented. Its organisational structure tends to be more flexible and changes fairly frequently and sometimes quite drastically. Achievement at work is more important than paper qualifications. Promotion can frequently be very rapid but there is little or no security of tenure. The more senior the job the less secure it is. Premature retirement and redundancy are not shied away from. If an idea, a new product or service, a new market, do not prove profitable, they are dropped without compunction. It is common to find men under forty in top positions. Profits are the criterion of success. Such firms tend to pay well. Sales staff in particular are well rewarded for success. Such firms often have a relatively high staff turnover and are prepared to recruit outside the firm to fill senior jobs. There is a high premium on blowing your own trumpet.

Family firms vary a great deal. Some are highly traditional. Others are at least as enterprising as the 'enterprise' type of firm. Some are very safety-conscious, and anxious to conserve what they have. Others, because the family is so wealthy, are prepared to take technical and financial risks that other companies would shy away from. Family firms are not all small. Some are extremely large. Some large publicly quoted companies with shares quoted on the Stock Exchange are still family companies.

The common characteristic of family companies is that they are controlled by one family or in some cases by two or three families, who are linked by long-standing ties. The most senior jobs are usually held by family members. The board room is dominated by family members and may even be the exclusive preserve of family members. Even so, some of the key decisions affecting the company may be made outside it, in the family drawing rooms. Young members of the family are encouraged to join the family firm. Even if they start at the bottom, their progress is accelerated. The style of the company is very much determined by the characters of the family members. Even one or two capable and determined family members can ensure a thrusting, go-ahead, profitable firm. The big weakness of such companies is the succession. So long as the family is determined to hold on to the top jobs, there is a danger that they will fall into the hands of family members who are pleasant but neither energetic nor capable. It is also common to find that family firms are unable to attract and retain good management talent because the top jobs are not open to non-family.

Of course, some families do realise the problem and introduce employees into the board room. Others go further and allow them real power and influence in the key decisions that affect the company. However at this stage they are starting to move away from family status.

Many family firms have a very good record for the paternalistic way in which they treat their staff. They look after those who are injured and the widows and families of men who die or are killed. They go beyond the limit of their legal liabilities. In the best family firms, the family members do take a genuine interest in their work people. Against this, they are frequently not the best payers. They sometimes resent trade unions. Often, they are not prepared to find capital for expansion, re-equipment or new development because it would involve diluting family control.

I have gone on about company styles at such lengths because the type of company you work for can have an important bearing on your promotion prospects and the way in which you plan for your promotion. Some people feel more at home in one style of company than in another. If you can, it probably pays to work for a company whose style matches your own inclinations.

HOW DOES YOUR COMPANY COMPARE WITH OTHERS?

It is not always easy to find out, but it is worth it. It is sensible to try to find out how it compares in terms of salaries, fringe benefits and promotion prospects with other firms. The younger you are the wider your net of comparisons should be. If you work in the private sector, you should also keep an eye on public sector salaries. They are more freely available for one thing. For another, you may be surprised at how well paid local and central government employees are despite all their propaganda to the contrary.

As part of the comparison process it is worth watching the job advertisements in the national press and in the trade or professional journals. For more junior jobs, it is possible to do your checking in the local papers. It is of course fine to look at the press advertisements and conclude that you would be better paid in another company. However you may be comparing your own job with one you would have no chance of getting. For many reasons, it may be a good idea, every two years or so, to select an advertised job and apply for it even if you have no intention of leaving your present company. If you are offered the job, it gives you a good fix on your market value. It may even give you a point of reference in discussions with your own company.

Apart from knowing how your company stands in relation to others in the field of pay and conditions, it is wise to try to find out how it stands generally in relation to other firms in the same field. This can have an important bearing on your future prospects. You can judge partly by your own knowledge of the company's products and how they compare with the opposition. By reading the trade press — and if the company is large enough, the national business press — you can get some feeling for the relative standing of your company.

Perhaps the most important source of information is their annual report and accounts. These may be fully reported in the quality press. Alternatively your bank manager will probably be prepared to obtain a copy for you, if you ask him. The important things to check are trends. Are your competitors increasing their share of the market? Is their profit and turnover per employee higher or lower than yours? Are they short of ready cash or do they appear to have a surplus of liquid funds? Are they increasing their employee numbers or decreasing them?

WHAT DOES IT MEAN FOR YOU?

Your may feel that I have put undue emphasis on knowing about your company. After all what does it matter, as long as they go on paying you? Well, it matters a lot. The company provides the environment in which you have to plan for your promotion.

In looking at your company, you should be trying to assess whether the company provides the opportunities which are needed to meet your aspirations. If it does not, do they provide some opportunity — sufficient to provide you with a springboard or are the opportunities so limited that you must change your job as soon as practicable?

If your company has a well defined system for promotion you need to examine the situation and see how you can improve your promotion prospects. If your company offers training facilities, ought you to be trying to get certain types of training to improve your prospects?

If you were going to make a journey through a wild jungle area, you would try to get a map or aerial photographs to help you find your way. If you hope to move along the promotion trail in the jungle of your company, you will find it a lot easier if you have a map. That map is the best possible understanding you can get of your own company and how it works.

12

Know Your Job

Know your job! You may think that is a silly piece of advice.
Of course you know your job now. You're doing it. In fact,
a great many people do not know their job. They continue
to do it in a routine way without thinking about it. In consequence, they do not do the job as well as it could be done
and fail to provide evidence of their suitability for promotion.

A very English man was travelling in the South West of
Ireland some time ago. He became lost and approached a
countryman. The conversation went like this: 'I say, do you
know the way to Kerry?' 'Yes' 'Can you tell me how to get
there?' 'Well if I was going myself, I wouldn't start from here.'
Unfortunately, when we start to plan our own promotion
path, we have to start from here. Normally, 'here' is our
present job. A good start is to know your present job really
well.

THINK ABOUT YOUR JOB

Some people, particularly those at the bottom of the ladder,
may reply: 'But my job is so dull and boring. That's the whole
point. There just is nothing to think about.' Well, I don't agree.

Even the dullest of jobs is worth thinking about. It is too easy to slip into a pattern where the job runs you instead of the reverse. You are governed by the intray and by the peple who chose to 'phone you or come into the office. In other lesser jobs you just do what the supervisor says or 'same as last time!'

In thinking about your job, the place to start is your statement of job objectives or your job description if you have one. Study them and consider whether you are doing the job, as specified. If you are not, why is this? Is it that you have forgotten that the job included certain tasks? Or even that you had not read the job specification before? Is there insufficient time to do the work? Or is the specification out of date, overtaken by events? Is it that some of the tasks are now done by someone else? This last is a bad sign because it either indicates that your boss feels you are not up to the job or has started to reduce the size of it. Or it means that someone else in the department is on the make and demonstrating his ability to get on with the job.

It is a salutary experience and also a wise precaution to go back to your job specification once a quarter. Read through it and consider how you are matching up to it. Try to have it kept up to date. Above all try to make sure that you are measuring up to it. In many companies, particularly large ones, you will be judged against the way you perform the tasks set out in your job specification and in particular how far you achieve any objectives set for your job.

Many companies work in a more muddled fashion. There are no job specifications and people's objectives are not spelt out. If you find yourself in this situation, it is a difficult one. It is of course possible to coast along and lead a comfortable life. However, your objective is to get on and you won't do this by coasting along. It is a truism that it is a lot easier to do something if you know what it is you are setting out to achieve. So, if you find yourself without a job specification, draft one for yourself. The most important part is the job purpose. This sets out the broad guidelines for the job. If an unusual problem occurs, it should be possible to approach it sensibly in the light of your job purpose. The advantage of a well drafted job purpose is that it does provide you with guidance as to why your job exists at all. With that guidance, you do not need to go and ask your boss what to do every time something unusual crops up.

Go on to set out your main tasks. The mere fact of writing them down will help to get your job clearer in your mind. Finally, who do you report to and who reports to you? This should be the easiest part. Unfortunately it sometimes is not. There can be situations where you are called on to work for one superior for one purpose and a second superior for another purpose. This sometimes works satisfactorily but more frequently it does not. Both superiors feel that they are not getting a fair share of your efforts. They may even feel that you try to trade one off against the other. In such cases it is worth trying to clarify in your own mind — and on paper — the extent of your responsibility to each boss.

Having worked out your own job specification, if you do not already have one, what do you do about it? The simple answer is to go along and see your boss with it. Discuss it with him and agree on any necessary modifications to your draft. Unfortunately life is not always simple. There are some old-fashioned managers who would regard it as an impertinence for a junior to do this. There are others, who do not like new ways and see no necessity for defining a job in this way. 'After all, everyone knows what the job entails. They always have done.'

In these circumstances it may be wise to keep the draft to yourself. Try to get it as clear as you can. If there are ambiguities, try and sort them out gradually by talking to your boss at suitable opportunities. There is no need to ask him outright if you don't want to. He can be led into talking about the particular point without a direct question. However, those who really are headed for the top of the pyramid have to learn early on to grasp nettles and not to be frightened off. An old-fashioned senior may huff and puff at your daring to produce a new-fangled job specification for yourself. Nonethe less he may still be impressed that you are bothering to think constructively about your job.

UNDERSTAND HOW AND WHY

You should understand how and why you do every part of your job. At the lowest level a real understanding of your job may enable you to do it more easily and to reduce the pressures on you. It may also be possible to make a material improvement, leading to greater efficiency and higher profit. The man who can do this on his own initiative is likely to draw attention to himself as a candiate for promotion.

'Why?' is the first and most important question to ask. The answer may be obvious but a superficial answer is not always the right one. Suppose, for instance, you work for a large organisation and your job is to get the bills out to your customers. What are you doing and why? Are you trying to get bills out with as few mistakes as possible? Are you doing it so that the customer knows how much he owes or what? I suggest that your objective is to get money owed to the organisation into its hands as early as possible. The majority of people do not pay bills until they receive them. Many people only pay bills a certain time after they receive them. They may pay their bills about a month after they receive them. They do so whether the bill is submitted promptly or is delayed for several weeks in the production.

If you are having every bill checked by someone other than the person who made it out, why do you do this? What is the result of doing so? How many mistakes are found? How many of those mistakes are made by the people making out the bills, because they knew it didn't matter if they made a mistake — the clever checker would find it.

To digress slightly, I once worked with a large organisation which used a computer to produce its bills. The computer was programmed to produce the bills in two groups. One group consisted of those the computer was concerned about for some reason. The second and very much larger group was those that the computer had no reason to suspect. Both piles of bills were collected by the accounts department each morning and taken away to another building some miles away. Both piles were then inspected. Each individual bill was inspected by a clerk, folded and put into an envelope for dispatch. At times bills were delayed for three or four weeks by this process.

Sometimes they were lost. The consequence was an unnecessary loss to the organisation of tens of thousands of
pounds a year — the interest on the money they failed to get
in promptly — not to mention the cost of employing people
to do work that was not necessary.

Why did this happen? Well, they always had checked the
bills. In the early stages, there had been teething troubles with
the computer. The department went on doing it 'just in case'.
The manager had failed to think about his job and did not ask
himself 'Why?'. The benefits of checking were minimal — very
few errors were found and the cost far outweighed the errors
found.

The moral is to ask yourself why you do everything in your
job, however basic. It is also worth understanding how everything is done. It can be embarrassing when a senior manager
arrives in your department, just as the staff are leaving. He
asks you to put something through right away and get it done
tonight as it's urgent. He stands there and waits for you to do
whatever is necessary. If you can go through the necessary
steps, he notes that you are on top of the job. If you flounder
and have to admit you don't know your way around your
own department and one of the simple repetitive tasks it does,
he will be annoyed because of the hold-up to his immediate
plans. He will also note your lack of grasp of your department's
duties.

An American-trained managing director was put into a
medium-sized manufacturing firm to save it from the disaster
that the major shareholders could see coming. He used to say
regularly to managers, when he met them: 'I don't want you
to work harder, just smarter'. If you are going to work smarter
you must understand how and why you do things and how
and why the people who work for you do things.

UNDERSTAND RELATIONSHIPS TO OTHER JOBS

You do not do your job in isolation. What you do depends
on the work of other departments in the company — and outside it for that matter. What you do also affects other departments and individuals in the company. You cannot fully

113

understand your own job unless you can also understand its relationship to these other departments.

The first thing to find out is which these departments are and who are the particular individuals in them who affect or are affected by your work. You ought of course to know already, but you may not — particularly if they are remote from you in another factory or office.

Examine all the material or information that comes to you. Is it in the form you need to do your job? Would it be helpful if it came to you in a different form or at a different time? If it would, why not go and discuss the matter with the person who supplies it to you? If you already know him, there is no problem. If you don't it may be sensible to mention your intention to your boss first, in case there is an element in the situation that he knows about and you don't. When you meet your supplier don't demand that he alters things to suit you. Tell him your problem and ask him if he can think of any way to solve the problem. With a little gentle leading, he may provide you with what you want. It may even make life easier for him too.

Similarly look at your output. Is a particular deadline or a method of packing awkward and expensive for you? Do you suspect that information you send out is of little or no use to the recipient? If so, go and see the people concerned and discuss their needs with them. If it is your job to meet the needs, then take trouble to understand what these needs are and work out how best to meet them.

If you have never met your opposite numbers in the departments which supply you and which you supply, you should try to put this right as soon as possible. If they work in the same location or even in the same town, this should be quite easy to arrange. If it means a long journey, a bit more preparation and justification will be needed.

Before going to see your opposite numbers, do your homework. Make sure you know the full connection between their work and yours. Know the facts about any recent disputes between your departments. Know about any recent special situations or problems. When you meet your opposite numbers do not try to reform the world in one visit. The essential is to establish a good relationship so that you can talk to them reasonably freely about mutual problems and ways in which you can help each other. However beware of being so vague that they wonder why you came and wasted their valuable time. Let them know that they are welcome to visit you if they want to.

If on some later occasion they take you at your word and arrive at an inconvenient time, make sure that you make them welcome and devote time to talking to them. If they have come from some distance give them a cup of tea or coffee and arrange for them to have lunch with you in your canteen or take them out with you to lunch, wherever you normally go. There is no need to pay for their meal though a drink will no doubt be appreciated. Remember the object of the exercise is to establish a good working relationship — nothing more and nothing less.

COULD YOU DO IT BETTER?

Unless you have been thinking about your job from the start, it is almost certain you can do it better. No job, however humdrum or routine, is completely static. The environment around it changes. New equipment becomes available. New techniques are developed. Even if your job was perfectly organised and done by your predecessor, time will have rendered it less than perfect.

In the course of thinking about your job and asking why you do things the way you do, you will almost certainly find ways that things can be done better; unnecessary duplication that can be avoided; even totally unnecessary work that can be dropped.

Having identified the places where things can be done better, set about steadily making the improvements. Where you, alone, are involved you can go straight ahead. Where other people are involved take things steadily. Think new ways of doing jobs right through. There is nothing worse than introducing a new method only to have to abandon it on the following day because of a major snag you had not foreseen. Explain the changes in advance. Discuss them with those concerned and obtain their advice and agreement. Use persuasion rather than trying to force things through. If someone produces a better idea or modification, adopt it. Don't stick to your original plan because it is your own.

Your present job is the base from which you will progress. You should try to demonstrate that you are really completely on top of it. There is of course one snag. If you are doing your job in a really first-rate manner there is a danger that you may become indispensible and your manager may block your promotion chances because he does not want to lose you. This is a purely defensive mechanism on his part and there is an easy way to deal with this problem.

Your manager's real concern is that if you leave him on promotion, he may have a problem filling your job, training the replacement and sorting out his mistakes. The way out for you, if you have one or more people working for you, is to groom one of them as your replacement. Train them up till they can do your job as well as you can do it yourself. When you go on holiday or on a course make sure that your manager sees that they can do the job and lets them do it.

This reduces your indispensibility and makes it possible, even advantageous, to promote you. As you progress up the ladder you should make it a firm rule always to select your successor from among those working for you. Train him up and try to make sure he gets your job when you are promoted. This has two additional advantages. You leave an ally in your old job, rather than a newcomer from some other department who might be tempted to make his name by being critical of your way of doing the job. Secondly you gradually build a reputation for being someone whom it is good to work for because you look after your staff and secure their promotion.

One of the principles of war is to operate from a secure base. Really knowing your job is one move towards forming a secure base. As you progress up the ladder it is necessary to repeat the process at each stage.

116

13

Your Plan

Most people who are managers or aspire to become managers
learn fairly early on that good things don't just happen. They
have to be planned for and worked for. Indeed, in making
plans, good managers allow for the perversity of the world.
This is summed up in Sam O'Donovan's law: 'If things can
go wrong, they will go wrong'. This is not as pessimistic as it
sounds. It is merely a warning that if you do want to get on
it is necessary to plan and to plan very carefully.

I do not rule out good luck. People do get lucky breaks
from time to time; breaks that are completely unplanned.
You must be flexible enough to take advantage of these
opportunities as they occur. They are not however a sub-
stitute for planning.

WHO IS RESPONSIBLE FOR YOUR DEVELOPMENT?

Before discussing your plan, I want to digress shortly on the
question of who is responsible for your development. If you
work for a good manager, he is likely to take an interest in
your development. He may discuss it with you and will
probably arrange some training for you, both on and off the
job.

In a large company, the personnel staff may well take an interest in your development. The firm may operate a manpower development plan. They may carefully index their staff so that when a vacancy occurs they are able to select just the right person to transfer or promote to fill the vacancy. If you enter a firm as an apprentice under a graduate entry scheme, or under any formal training system, there will probably be some manager who is designated to watch over your development and progress.

However, despite all these good fairies watching over you, remember that when the chips are down, there is really only one person fully responsible for your development and that is yourself. In any organisation people move about, leave and are promoted. If you rely on someone else for your development, you may be left in the lurch. Your promotion plans may suffer a setback and someone else, who has not relied heavily on other people to develop him, may beat you to the post.

If there are other people who see themselves as responsible for your development, fine. This is obviously a helpful bonus. It may also be a means of getting a second opinion on your prospects and on those parts of your plan that you care to disclose. For myself, I prefer to keep my real plans close to my chest, and only check on the feasibility of specific points with anyone who considers himself responsible for me.

In the end, there is only one person who can plan for your promotion and carry the plan into effect. That is yourself. If you fail to recognise this, you are likely to spend your forties and fifties stranded on the lower slopes of the pyramid of your organisation bitter and disillusioned. The junior or middle manager with a kingsize chip on his shoulder because he has not reached his full potential has no-one to blame but himself.

Circumstances change. Companies merge and are taken over. Products and services become obsolete and are superceded. People will always be treated unfairly. Some people will always get an unfair advantage. Some people who are cheats, charlatans or even criminals will prosper. That unfortunately is the way of the world. This is, however, no reason for your failure.

Excuses, yes; but excuses can always be found for any failure. As the old Hindu proverb has it 'Stumbling is the excuse of a lame horse'. It is better to face up to your own responsibility for your own future than to spend your later life making excuses or finding scapegoats.

As children we get into the habit of relying on others to plan our future development. We depend on our parents and on school teachers. It can be a lasting habit. This is recognised in the modern educational approach of setting out alternative courses before children but leaving final decisions to them. In any case, once we have left school or university and entered adult life, we need to adopt adult ways. The mature adult is self-dependent. He recognises his own responsibility for his own development.

So, whatever you want to do with your life, the responsibility for doing it and for developing yourself in such a way as to make it possible is your own.

OBJECTIVES, SHORT-TERM TARGETS

The man who plans his activity normally achieves more than the one who doesn't. This is just as true of the professional golfer or boxer as it is of the businessman, public servant or surgeon. The first task in any plan is to define the objective.

Your objective is what you hope to achieve. If you know what you hope to achieve you must have a better chance of achieving it than if you don't. Most of us, however careful we are at planning at work, tend to baulk at planning our own lives. We have very muddled objectives. This is because we want a little of everything and do not think about it sufficiently clearly. We want to be happy, enjoy life with our family, do well, earn more money, be well thought of, better, greatest . . . and so on.

This is all too vague. Take a simple case. Suppose your objective is one of those mentioned. You want to earn more money. But how much more? And by when? If your objective is more money, it is better to express it in concrete terms. For instance, to earn £3000 a year by the age of 25, £4500 by 30 and £12,000 a year by 40. You then have a concrete target to aim for and a quantitative means of judging what, in due course, you have achieved against target.

If you do want to express your objectives in financial terms, there is of course the problem of inflation. The man who in 1962 had the objective of earning £4000 a year by 1976 would not have achieved that target in real terms if in fact he earned £4000 in 1976. Inflation would mean that his performance against target was very poor. So if you express your objectives in financial terms set them in current money terms and adjust for inflation.

When deciding what it is you want to do with your life, there is a strong case for setting both long-term objectives and short-term targets that are compatible with the objectives. I joined the Army during the war and my personal objective was to become a sapper officer. I really worked at it. Despite a number of setbacks, I managed to get my commission after a year and a half. I then sat back on my laurels and drifted. It was years before I reassessed my future and set myself fresh objectives. In this, I was not unique. A great many professional men set themselves the objective of qualifying in their profession and are content to let things drift when they qualify. Some graduates leaving university take it half a step further. They are content to graduate and secure a job in a substantial organisation.

All these people make the same mistake as I did. They work for years towards a clear-cut objective which they achieve with relief. They have seen a proportion of their fellow students fall by the wayside and this strengthens their relief and pride in their own achievement. What they fail to realise is that what they have achieved is only the first rung on the ladder. If they pause too long on the first rung, others will pass on their way up. After a time they become so attached to the bottom rung that they cannot move away from it.

Not everyone wants to get to the top of the pyramid. This is probably just as well, as there isn't much room at the top. Even those who want to get to the top may have different ideas of what constitutes the top man in a fairly small company rather than earn very much more by being a couple of levels from the top of a much bigger company. Some people prefer to be the head of a particular technical or specialist branch of a company rather than go to the top of the whole company. Nor is this just a rationalisation of failure. Not every Finance Director or Chief Engineer would enjoy doing the work his Managing Director does.

Equally, not everyone wants to get onto the administrative or management ladder. They prefer to exercise and perfect their own particular skills. It may be much better that they do. It is a commonplace of business life that disaster frequently follows the appointment of the best salesman to fill the job of sales manager.

It is a very difficult task to clarify your long-term objectives, but it is unlikely that you will ever fully develop your own potential unless you do clarify them. It takes time and thought to do so. It is very easy to drift into day-dreaming on the subject. In these circumstances one ends up with woolly objectives or a set of platitudes, like the parson who was 'agin sin'.

In the process of clarifying one's long-term objectives it helps to write them down. At first shot you may end up with a long rambling paragraph of good intentions. Gradually it must be refined until you have a clear unambiguous statement.

In setting your own long-term objectives, it is important to be realistic. By this I do not mean that you should be unambitious. It is perfectly realistic for a school-leaver, joining a company to make becoming its managing director his objective. A cadet joining the police force can reasonably aim to become a chief constable. But it is unrealistic for a forty year old clerk, who has just joined a giant firm like Unilever, Shell or ICI, to think that he has any chance of becoming managing director. To get on in any large organisation takes time. To qualify in any profession takes time. To start out in middle life to rectify lack of qualifications and progress is perfectly possible, but the highest posts, in general, are probably not attainable in the time that remains.

There is of course a notable exception. Many people have decided in middle age that they are getting nowhere in life as employees and launch out on their own. Some have

founded very successful companies and have achieved both
wealth and satisfaction in the process. If anything, they
have needed an even clearer view of their objectives than
anyone setting out to achieve success as an employee.

Once you have decided on your objectives, which may
take twenty or more years to achieve, think about the
immediate stages. Twenty years is a long time and if the
objectives are to be attained it is necessary to have shorter-
term targets. These are necessary to maintain your morale
and interest. They are also necessary to help you pace the
course and measure progress. If you joined the Army with
the intention of becoming a general, there are a number of
well defined intermediate steps which must be achieved.
These include promotion to the various intermediate ranks
and passing promotion exams. There are also less well
defined requirements. A certain type of training and
experience may be required at various stages. Annual reports
must reflect a certain quality of performance. The right
impression must have been made in different places and at
different times. Most bureaucratic organisations have a
similar pattern.

In smaller firms and in fluid enterprising firms, the steps
will be much less well defined. Nonetheless you must try to
identify intermediate targets. It is not necessary to identify
intermediate targets all the way across twenty years or more.
Indeed it would be totally unrealistic to do so. There is,
however, a considerable advantage in having identified, at
least, the next two steps.

The next step should, ideally, be attainable within the next
two years and preferably within one. This gives you something
immediate to aim for. You can plan and work in detail for a
target which you can see clearly in front of you and which
you know you can make.

If you have also set the next target beyond the immediate
one, this helps you to keep up the momentum after you
achieve the first target. Each time you achieve a target, this
should trigger a review of your plan to make sure that it is
realistic and on course. You should also ensure that at least
the next two targets are set.

When you first start planning your promotion, your early

targets may be expressed in terms of your job. For instance, if you are a salesman you may set your target in terms of producing sales at a level 25 per cent above the target set for you by the company. Similarly, a branch manager may aim to exceed his turnover or profit contribution by 10 per cent over the company target. A production manager may set his own target in terms of reducing waste, increasing turnover or improving productivity. Targets of this sort should be set in terms, which if achieved, will be meaningful to your manager and draw attention to your ability to do your job not just satisfactorily, but well.

In some fields you may feel that the first essential if you are to get on is to get either an initial qualification or some additional one. This can appear a formidable obstacle. If you are a non-graduate and see that 90 per cent of all senior and middle managers in your organisation are graduates, you may well conclude that it is essential to obtain a degree as a first step in your promotion plan. This would be difficult, but not impossible. Totally unqualified people can obtain a degree from the Open University in six years of part-time study and an honours degree with an additional two years of study. The really dedicated who are prepared to devote twenty hours a week or more to study can obtain their degree in three years with a further year for an honours degree.

Most of us tend to be unambitious in setting ourselves targets. We prefer to set targets we are sure of being able to achieve. This can be a mistake. If you are going to achieve something with your life, you will need to push yourself. I set myself targets which I think are a little bit more than I can achieve in the time. If I make them, I am pleased. If I take an extra few months, I don't worry about it.

Once I have determined a long-term objective and set the first two intermediate targets, I try to plan in detail how I will achieve the first of these targets. To do this I set out step by step what work I have to do. I make out a timetable showing what will be done in each week between now and the target date. I put as much as possible in the early weeks and try to plan for 3 or 4 weeks contingency. There are weeks which I leave free in my plan to allow me to catch up lost time and to cover anything I have overlooked at the planning stage.

CONSIDER ALTERNATIVES

In making your promotion plan, don't accept too easily that there is only one possible objective for you. Even more, once you have set your objectives and first two intermediate targets, don't assume that there is only one way of getting there. There may be one obvious route, the one that everyone else has chosen and followed in the past. It isn't necessarily the only route.

You certainly shouldn't take this for granted. It is always worth looking for the less obvious ways of achieving your objectives. These will have the advantage of originality and will keep your competitors guessing. Hard slogging work is effective in producing results. But good thinking generally produces more profitable results more quickly than hard sweat.

It will be easier to consider the alternatives if you write them down with their advantages and disadvantages. Once you have written them down, you can go back to them after a few days and judge them more objectively. After a break of this sort you will be able to see the gaps more easily and the advantages and disadvantages more clearly.

BE TRUE TO YOURSELF

Polonius gave his son, Laertes, much excellent advice. Perhaps best of all was his comment: 'This above all: To thine own self be true. And it must follow, as the night the day, thou cans't not then be false to any man.'

If you are really determined, you can get to the top, but you should consider your motives very carefully. Do you really want to get to the top — whatever the cost? Don't fool yourself into thinking there is no cost. It is easy to concentrate on the outward trappings of power. You can see these clearly. What you can see less clearly is the dedicated effort, the sacrifice of family life, hobbies and friends. For many people, the route to the top is pursued in partnership with a spouse, equally dedicated to their success. The spouse may be happy to subordinate her interests totally to the advancement of her partner. Even in these cases, there has to be a concentration on the main chance and some narrowing of interests and horizons.

You can of course argue, that many people get in a rut in early years anyway. Shortage of interest and of money reduces them to automatons who follow the daily grind and lose themselves in front of the TV every night. At the weekend, they relax with a shopping trip and polishing the car in the drive. In such cases, would very much except idleness be sacrificed to a more determined approach to career development. In such cases career development may widen and develop interests rather than the reverse. It may help to create a more interesting person with a wider range of friends and acquaintances.

In a way the test of a career comes at the end — when you look back on it. Was it a barren futile struggle? Were the fruits of success tasteless and unsatisfying? Or was it all a satisfying and enjoyable journey?

Another question that arises is what means are you prepared to adopt in your journey towards the top? Are you always going to do what is fair and decent? Will you stay not only within the law but within the dictates of conscience and any moral law you recognise? Will you play by Queensberry rules and rely entirely on your own merits and constructive efforts to get to the top? I would guess that few people reach the very top without a touch of guile and a touch of ruthlessness. If a friend goes through a bad patch and is not doing his job effectively, do you go out of your way to help him and cover for him or do you ignore his problems? Worse, will you step on him to give yourself a lift up? If the managing director insists on cuts being made, do you carry out his wishes and ruthlessly throw out those who are no longer up to ever-increasing standards? Do you carry out policies which, in your heart, you believe are unfair?

Many people may say that the end does not justify the means. They reach a sticking point where they prefer to do

what is, in their view, right rather than that which seems
expedient in the race to the top. It sometimes happens,
in doing what is right, that they still come through and integrity
pays off. Don't bank on it though. The real world is a nasty
rough tough place. The determined search for power and
influence has led many people into corrupt and ruthless
ways. As James Russell Lowell wrote:

'Little he loved, but power the most of all
And that he seemed to scorn, as one who knows
By what foul paths men choose to crawl thereto.'

Many fool themselves by saying that when they get to the
top they will make restitution. That is not easy.

It is of course always possible to exaggerate the extent to
which others may stray from the path of rectitude. I once
belonged to a writers organisation and went along to two of
their meetings. Whenever anyone present referred inadvert-
ently to successful writers, they immediately and hurriedly
qualified 'by successful I mean of course materially
successful'. To write a book that more than 1500 people
might want to buy was seen as something suspect. One can
become concerned with purity to the extent of losing touch
with reality.

To consider all these questions is not just to moralise. It
is to point out that there may be things in life more valuable
to you than material success and power. If there are, do not
be afraid to recognise the fact even if it means you have to
be content to end on a lower rung of the ladder than the
top; you may be happier there. Further, if you really are
'star quality' you may still get to the top with a clear
conscience.

14

Your Boss

Perhaps the single most important factor affecting your promotion, outside yourself, is your boss, or more correctly your boss and your relationship with him. What your boss thinks of you has a very great bearing on your future. Quite apart from promotion, he can make your life easy or difficult, as he chooses.

When I was a very young officer in the Army, I was sent to collect a piece of expensive machinery, a special generator, from a depot some 200 miles away. It was in Germany just after the 1939-45 war. I went by car and took a lorry with a corporal in charge of it. Instead of going to the depot I made a detour to another town to deal with a private matter of my own. I met the corporal back at our own camp. When the generator was unloaded, it was found to be unserviceable. The technical adjutant decided it was damaged because of the way it had been loaded in the lorry. He discovered that I had not supervised the loading and set out to gun for me. I had clearly been guilty of a number of misdemeanors or crimes, for which I could have been court martialled. Fortunately for me, I had done some effective work over the previous few months and my commanding officer had formed a favourable impression of me. The whole affair was quietly forgotten.

You may think that what happened in the post-war Army is not a reliable guide to the situation in a modern company. My own observation is that human nature is much the same, wherever you find it. Most bosses have a fairly wide discretion. In practise, in the modern industrial and commercial corporation, your boss probably has a lot more discretion than Army officers who are firmly bound by regulations.

THE KEY TO YOUR FUTURE

Your boss is the key to your future in many ways. He will review your salary and make any recommendations for increase. If your firm give any fringe benefits, he will be consulted before any new benefits are extended to you. He will put your name forward for further training, for transfers or for promotion. In some firms, he can block your progress so effectively, if he so chooses, that progress becomes impossible for you. In such circumstances you have to move to another company or resign yourself to waiting for your boss to move on or die.

If you are tempted to take the easy way and wait for him to go, beware. If you stay for a long time under a boss who is determined to block you, his influence will extend way beyond his departure. If he has given you a bad name it will stick. His reports, his judgements and the view of you which he hands over will dog you for some time to come.

In some cases there are opportunities which will only discover if your boss chooses to tell you.

It is interesting to note that people sometimes move upwards in a group. The key man builds a group around him. As he is promoted so he gradually moves the members of the group into jobs around him. There seems to be a symbiotic relationship. The key man needs the loyal henchmen to support him and prepare the situation which will lead to his next promotion. They, in turn, only rise because of his patronage.

It is not always a group that advances in this way. It may sometimes be a pair who complement each other well. Movements of this sort happen at all levels of a hierarchy, though it is more obvious as you get near the top of a pyramid. I have seen a man, who was himself severely lacking in management quality rise to the senior levels of a nationalised undertaking by attaching himself to a man, of much greater ability, whom he had known well at university.

I have heard of cases where a man has moved into another company as chairman or managing director. He has been followed within a few months by two or three henchmen. A few months later, the henchmen bring in their own henchmen to important posts. These posts are either newly created or made vacant by harrying existing incumbents.

This matter of group movements is another story. It is however sensible to note the importance of groups in the promotion race. A key factor in any group is the leader, which brings us back to the original point — the importance of your boss. You may think that your boss will have less influence over your future as you move up a hierarchy; this is not so. The higher up you move, the more critical your relationship with your boss becomes.

STUDY AND ANALYSE YOUR BOSS

It is not necessary to like your boss or even to respect him, though clearly this helps. It is important that you know him; that you know what makes him tick; that you know what his prejudices and pet hates are. It is also desireable to build up a picture of his contacts. This last may seem a minor point. Yet some years ago I knew a senior manager in a Midlands engineering firm. His wife and three daughters all worked as secretaries in the firm. His three sons-in-law also worked in the firm. They were well spread through the firm and he consequently had an excellent information network. The range of information and comment he picked up was quite surprising.

Information about what you do and say can filter back to your boss along any number of routes. If you are in the habit of making indiscrete comments, it is as well to know the extent of your boss's circle of cronies. The tentacles of his information network may stretch into some strange places.

In planning your promotion, it is essential to know your boss. You need to ensure that he does not hinder you. Perhaps more important, you need to calculate how he might help you. The best way to do this is to watch what he does; study his behaviour. Remember the man is best judged by what he does rather than what he says. Bark and bite do not always coincide. The fact that a man has a photograph of his wife and children in his office does not necessarily mean that he is a happily married man. One such manager that I came across always had a colour photograph of his wife and children prominently displayed on his desk and his secretary was his mistress!

A manager may throw his weight about in conversations with his subordinates, yet be a complete yes-man when talking to his own superiors. If you have the opportunity to observe your manager with his superiors, it is instructive. Is he able to put his points across and secure any necessary agreement from his seniors? If there is blame to be accepted, does he accept it himself, or does he shuffle it on to his subordinates? Is he easy in his relationships with them or does he clearly irritate them?

In fact is is very important to know the standing of your boss and what weight he carries in the company. In many companies the size of a man's office, the luxury of its furniture and fittings and the appearance of his secretary give an indication of his standing. But be careful, appearances may be deceptive. These outward trappings of power may indicate a situation that has existed in the past. They may no longer indicate the reality of the situation.

It is also true that some organisations give very plush offices to their front men who deal with the less important but status-conscious outside world. This may be the case for instance with the manager who sifts crank inventors, handles the more vociferous public complaints or deals with Government or local town officials. The trappings are an essential setting for his job, not an indication of his power and influence in the firm.

Bosses vary a great deal in the amount of themselves they disclose to their subordinates. But you can still observe him carefully at work. Does he give clear and explicit instructions? Does he set objectives? If he does, are they realistic? Does he check to see that they are achieved? Is he willing to listen or is he a monotonous pontificator? Does he take two hours to say what might be said in ten minutes more effectively? Does he concentrate his attention on essentials? Does he devote time to inessentials or to things which he believes affect his status or standing? Does he have moods? Are some times better than others for approaching him with new ideas? If a report or paper is put before him does he read it for its meaning or for its spelling and grammatical mistakes?

Mr Jones was a senior manager in a large electronics firm. In his day he had been an innovative engineer, but by the age of fifty, not unnaturally, his engineering knowledge was dated. He used to receive formal written reports from his managers every four weeks. These reports, together with a brief summary written by himself, then formed his report to his director. The reports related to technical activities and to the putting into practice of the firm's technical policies, yet it was noticeable that Mr Jones rarely, if ever, queried the substance of the report. He would happily spend twenty minutes discussing how to avoid a split infinitive. The end product was an unusually literate business report. He put great weight on judging his subordinates, upon their ability to write grammatically correct reports. Those of his subordinates, who wished to progress, knew that in practice it was important to devote extra time to polishing their report-drafting and re-drafting it and checking spelling against the dictionary. They did this at the expense of their work, which may have had longer run disadvantages to their company. However, they knew their manager and applied their knowledge to obtain benefit for themselves in the pay and promotion stakes.

Some managers have a considerable interest in outside activities. These may be sporting, artistic, professional or technical. Other things being equal those of his subordinates who also participate in these activities or are at least knowledgeable about them are likely to have the edge over their colleagues. Some managers make a point of not having lunch with their subordinates. Others do lunch with people who work for them. If your manager sits next to you at lunch from time to time, it is obviously an easier and more profitable occasion if you can talk about his favourite subject — or at least listen intelligently while he talks.

Some managers are keen to receive outward signs of

respect. They are, perhaps, found most often in family firms or commercial bureaucracies. They like their subordinates to knock at their office door before entering. They like them to stand up if they visit the subordinate in his own office though they tend to summon subordinates to their own office rather than visit them in their own humble surroundings. These managers like to be addressed as 'Sir' and generally accorded the old fashioned courtesies. Despite their protestations to the contrary, many career women managers are also keen on the conventional courtesies.

Other managers are the reverse. They don't care about their subordinate's manners so long as they produce results. They do not want yes men. They want people with good ideas who will not be afraid of them. Nonetheless, at the end of the day, most managers do expect their subordinates to defer to them. Your manager may well have different attributes. The main point is to identify those attributes as early as possible.

MODEL YOURSELF ON YOUR BOSS

Given that your boss and his attitude to you are key factors in your future, what can you do about it? The first thing is to establish to your own satisfaction that you are reasonably compatible. If the very sight of you brings forth his enmity and scorn, you should start planning a move away from his sphere of interest as soon as possible.

In the vast majority of cases, the situation will not be as bad as this. You may not like him, but at least you can get on with him if you try. In these circumstances, I suggest you should model yourself on him and his ideas. By this I do not mean that your behaviour should be a cheap imitation of his. Rather it should complement his.

If he is a fiend for punctuality, be punctual. You may think that the managing director who starts work in the office every morning at 7.30 a.m. is going a bit far. There is no need to join him at that hour unless he asks you. However, if the office officially opens at 9 a.m. each day, it is tactless to arrive regularly between 9.10 and 9.20. The MD, if he wants to ask

132

you a question, may well wait fairly patiently from 7.30 to just before 9. By ten past he may well be spitting with rage. Even a results-oriented MD is likely to expect his headquarters staff to keep office hours compatible with his. Indeed, one problem can be keeping up with an effective manager who is dedicated to his work and puts in long hours.

From your knowledge of your own manager, try to build a picture in your own mind of what he expects from you. Part of this may be in your formal objectives. Some of his expectations may be informal requirements in terms of behaviour and attitudes. If he is a High Tory in his politics and you are a keen socialist, you do not have to abandon your political beliefs, but you may be wise to keep off politics in the office and to avoid political comments to him. You may enjoy a discussion of a political nature with him, and you may score some points. However, unless you are good personal friends — a rare situation in business — you are best advised to keep off. You will do yourself more harm than good.

Almost anyone has some prejudices. You may even have one or two yourself. Watch out for your bosses' predjudices and avoid kicking them.

Most bosses, as part of their job, try to identify their successor and to identify people suitable for promotion within the firm. In doing so, they inevitably measure their people against some standard. In part this may be an objective standard in terms of qualifications, experience and achievements. A major part of this standard will however be based on his informal picture of the ideal manager. More often than not, that is someone cast in the same mould as himself.

If you want to be seen as a man suitable for promotion, it may pay you to play down your differences from your boss and to emphasise your points of similarity. Be careful however. People do not always see themselves as others see them. The manager whom you see as an indecisive ditherer, may well see himself as a dynamic decisive leader.

NEVER STAB YOUR BOSS IN THE BACK

You may sometimes be tempted to stab your boss in the back,

figuratively speaking. The opportunity may arise to show him up in a bad light. You may be able to demonstrate his fault or incapacity in public. You may have a chance to score him off in front of his boss. If you are standing in for him when he is ill or on holiday, you may have the opportunity to demonstrate his incompetence.

There are myriad ways in which you can stab your boss in the back. My advice is 'Don't'. I say this not purely from humanitarian motives but for the simple reason that it very rarely pays. You may do it when you are about to leave the company. You might even risk giving him the final stab when his boss has already set him up for destruction. On the whole I believe it is wiser to exercise restraint. If you really dislike your boss and find you can not work satisfactorily with him, it is much better to move away.

I once watched an interesting situation. Mike had worked for his boss Henry for many years. He owed quite a lot to Henry's patronage. They were fellow freemasons and spent quite a lot of time in each others company. The boss consulted Mike about his work and his decisions. He sometimes let his hair down in discussing the director to whom he reported. The director was replaced by a bright young import from outside the company who was determined to change everything very quickly. As part of this process he started to put pressure on the managers who reported to him. He wanted extra jobs done as well as demanding revised plans and budgets. He called for special reports with tight deadlines. Henry discussed the new arrangements very fully with Mike. Mike could see how things were going. He realised that the new director intended to have change and was putting the skids under Henry. At this stage, Mike, as well as trying to ingratiate himself with the new director, started to give Henry bad advice. He fed Henry, who was only too receptive, with all the quibbles and objections he could. He egged him on to being obstructive to the new director. It didn't take long for the crunch to come. Henry was removed from his job. However he had been in the company for a long time and still had some powerful friends. A job was found for him in another division.

Mike took over Henry's job, but it was made clear that it was only an acting post. Everyone else in the department realised what had happened. Henry had been liked as a pleasant man to work for. Mike's part in the affair was resented. Several other senior people in the department started to apply for jobs elsewhere in the company. Mike found it even more difficult to meet the director's demands than Henry had. He lasted about three months. A replacement was brought in from outside the company and Mike was declared redundant.

People will happily grumble away about their boss, but they do not like to see him knifed. This is particularly so as he has been a figure in all their pay and promotion hopes. Mike had misread the situation. If he had loyally supported him Henry might still have been moved in due course. At that stage Mike would probably have been given the job. He would have come in with the support of his colleagues and a fighting chance of success. As it was, Mike was not tough enough and not good enough at the job to survive. In stabbing his boss, he also destroyed himself.

15

Help Your Boss

We have seen how important your boss is to your future. What will persuade him to help you? I have heard of cases, where men set out to annoy their bosses to such an extent that the boss recommended them for promotion just to get rid of them.

This is unusual. In most cases your boss will recommend your promotion if he believes you are worth it. He is more likely to think you are worth it if he has formed a favourable impression of you.

DON'T WASTE HIS TIME

The first and most important way in which you can help your boss is to refrain from wasting his time. Every manager doing a worth-while job is pressed for time. There is always more work for him to do than he has time for. He copes with the situation by not doing some of the work and by delegating some.

Some people like to run to their boss whenever anything unusual happens. They are continuously seeking his advice and providing him with odd titbits of information. They feel that being in frequent contact with their boss must be a good thing. If out of sight means out of mind, they argue that it is important to keep yourself in the boss's eye.

When the boss is in the office, they try and get in to see him at least once in the day. Whenever his secretary relaxes her vigilance or leaves her place, they nip in with 'just a quick point'. If the boss is away from the office, they pursue him with telephone calls and telex messages. In their over-enthusiasm to keep the boss in the picture, they phone the poor man when he is at home or on holiday. Poor boss. He is trying to get on with his own job. He does not want to act as a permanent nanny to his staff. He wants them to think for themselves and get on with it. There are occasions when he must be told of events immediately. Before you disturb him, ask yourself, 'What can he do about it?' If the answer is 'Nothing', is it worth disturbing him?

If you do have to tell your boss something or ask his advice, try to do it in an organised way which will cause the minimum disruption to his day. If he sees you regularly once a day, once a week or once a month, will the point wait till you see him at your next regular meeting? If you give him a formal written report at regular intervals, can it be covered in the next report?

In saying all this, do not let yourself be frightened away from seeing the boss if you really have to see him about something. However, if you have to pop your head into his office half a dozen times a day or if you can not let a day go past without talking to him, I suggest that in most cases this is a sign that something is wrong and the situation needs review.

The main exception to the general rule is when the work that you and your boss do is closely interlinked and you both need to know the up-to-date position. This may happen if you are working together on a report or the design of a new product. It will happen more frequently if your boss is a project manager rather than a line manager. Where a boss needs to work so closely with one or more subordinates, they may share an office or have interconnecting ones.

The general rule remains valid; don't disturb your boss unless you need to. If you do need to do so, try to do it at a

Don't disturb your boss unless you need to

time which is convenient to him, rather than at the time it is easiest for you.

More important, be prepared when you do go to see him. Have clear in your own mind what you want from your discussion with the boss. Why do you want to see him? What do you expect to achieve from seeing him? Have you information to give him? If so marshall it logically. Give him as much background as he needs to be given to enable him to grasp the significance of the information. Don't wander from the point.

If you want a decision from him, ask yourself what factors affect the decision and what information he will need to make it. If the matter is at all complicated, it will probably pay to put it in writing. This helps you to organise the material into a logical sequence and consequently makes it easier for your boss to understand. Also, if it is a complicated matter try to leave the boss enough time to study the matter. Don't take it to him at the eleventh hour, so that he has to drop everything else. He may become so annoyed that he gives the 'wrong' or inconvenient decision in these circumstances out of sheer cussedness.

Do you sometimes go helplessly to your boss with a problem and just dump it in his lap? It helps him and develops you to consider the problem for yourself. You may still have to go to the boss even if you can solve the problem for yourself. The solution may involve expenditure or decisions beyond your authority. It is still best to go to the boss with the problem and with a suggested solution. In the case of a difficult problem, it may be better still to go to him with two or more solutions together with a statement of the arguments for and against. In this case you should always be prepared to make a firm recommendation and to give your reasons. You won't get to the top by sitting on the fence.

Be careful that you do not make a mountain out of a molehill. If you can solve the problem and have the authority to do so, don't bother the boss. Try not to worry him about non-management problems and do not produce a weighty case to deal with a trivial problem. If you spend half an hour making a case for buying HB pencils instead of 2H you are unlikely to earn his thanks or respect.

Some people send their boss a copy of every memo and letter they write. Just to be on the safe side, they write an office memo recording their telephone conversations and send him a copy of those as well. The boss has several courses open to him. He can read them all. He can put them in the pending basket, throw them away or place an intermediate level of management between you and him. Any one of these courses can be disastrous for you.

There are still a few old fashioned managers who wish to see everything that is written in their division or department. This is increasingly unusual. A good manager will tell you what he wants to see. This may include letters of a non-routine nature to suppliers or customers and internal office memos going to people of equal or greater standing than him in the organisation.

When you start a new job it is worth discussing with the boss what he needs to see. If you take over a job, or are doing one now, where copies of everything or nearly everything go to the boss, think about it. How much does he really need? What will he do as a result of reading it? If the answer in a large number of cases is nothing, then do a proper review of the situation. Classify your written output and try to identify the types of written material you produce which your boss really needs to see. Put a firm proposal to your boss for cutting down the papers which go to him. Depending on your relationship with your boss and the number of classes of paper, put it to him orally or in writing. If necessary, sound him out gently first or try him out on a particular type of letter.

Another technique is to stop the flow of paper to him gradually. In the early stages of such a compaign it is as well to mention in passing that you have written to X but haven't bothered him with a copy. You will soon get a feel for his reaction and an indication of how quickly and directly you can correct the paper flow.

Most managers face a problem with the amount of written material they have to skim through. Anything you can do to reduce his paperwork is likely to be appreciated by your boss. Apart from cutting down on the habit of sending him a copy of everything 'just in case' there are a number of other ways you can help. Do you forward to him reports and detailed papers from your subordinates and others? It is all too easy to mark such papers for the boss 'to see'. It is more work for you to summarise them in a short covering note to the boss. This can take the form of a summary of the points relevant to your boss, highlighting the information he needs or drawing attention to those points that require decision or action from him. Alternatively you can mark the key passages or give the references in your note.

Whatever you do, keep it simple and avoid being fussy or pedantic. Remember the object of the exercise is to help your boss save his time. It is not to conceal unwelcome news from him but to enable him to use his time effectively.

Many people in your company and outside will want to deal with your boss rather than with you. Some of them will want to do so, simply because he is the senior man. They want to visit him, or talk to him or write to him or get him to their meetings because of his seniority. In some cases this may be justified, but in many others the subject matter lies wholly within your responsibility and competence. If your boss gets involved, two of you will be devoting your time to the meeting. The time your boss spends on the matter will be a waste. Try to demonstrate your competence to these people. Tactfully try to head them off from the boss and equally tactfully make it clear to the boss that you can cope.

THAT LITTLE EXTRA

Another way you can help your boss is to be prepared to do that little extra. Some awkward jobs crop up in any department. Perhaps a routine report is due out and the man who normally prepares it goes sick. If the boss asks you if you can handle it, get on and do it. Don't waste half an hour telling him you are too busy to do it.

Perhaps an overseas customer or trade mission is visiting the company and it falls to your department to keep them happy at the weekend. If the boss asks you to show them around the local beauty spots, do it cheerfully. Try and make a good impression on the visitor and send them away happy. Don't as some people do, get your own back by caning your expenses.

There can be many occasions, particularly at the start of your career, when your boss needs someone to come into the office early, leave late or work over a weekend or public holiday. Be prepared to do it. If your boss develops a picture of you as keen and willing, it is likely to be to your advantage.

Old soldiers say 'never volunteer for anything'. I think this is poor advice. When I was a young soldier at an engineering officer cadet school, I wasn't too bright and generally didn't do well in the theoretical tests. Whenever a volunteer was needed to jump in the lake to hold or lift a piece of bridging, I was always first in — with a big splash. It paid off. Despite being on the commandant's mat after all but one of the 'block tests', I still made it. The fact that I was observed to be prepared to have a go at the unpleasant jobs clearly helped.

I believe that it pays to be prepared to have a go at the awkward jobs in any walk of life. It happens, sometimes, that you will take on a difficult job which everyone else backs off because they think it is impossible to do within the constraints laid down. By the time you have completed the job successfully within your terms of reference, the problems have been rationalised away in the other people's minds. You did it, so it clearly wasn't that difficult. If this happens to you, all you can do is to put it down to experience. If you can see the possibility of it happening from the start of the job, try to get some benefits in the early stages — like a pay rise, promotion or extra fringe benefits. Most Englishmen, traditionally, are slow to take advantage of a situation such as this to negotiate a better deal for themselves. Americans are less inhibited. Many of them start a new or awkward job by agreeing the objectives and terms of reference they will have and then go straight into negotiating better pay and conditions of service for themselves. There is a lot to commend this approach, but not every boss will appreciate it; some might even turn nasty.

The general case remains valid. If by putting yourself out you can help the boss, it is normally sensible to do so. It is likely to result in a better atmosphere between you and your boss. It should also enhance both pay and promotion prospects.

Within large organisations, there may be much jockeying for position. This may sometimes involve every section or department trying to avoid accepting responsibility for awkward or difficult tasks. When your boss is finally landed with the job and passes it on to you, it may involve your whole section putting themselves out to do the job. It is still worth your while to take it on, but see that some of the credit and reward rubs off on the people who do the work.

There may be many minor personal ways in which you can help the boss. If his car goes in for repair, he may be glad of a lift home or to the garage. If you travel abroad there may be some item he wants or some personal message delivered. It shows willing if you ask whether there is anything you can do for him while you are away. Similarly if he is going away for a trip abroad, ask if there is anything you can do for him while he is away. If he telexes or phones you to say when he will be arriving home, be sure to let his wife know, though you had best make sure that he intends to go straight home to his wife and not dally elsewhere on the way. However you should know him well enough to gauge this anyway.

HELP HIM TO DELEGATE

There is one major way in which you can do a little extra to help your boss. Accept delegation of some of his work. Don't just accept it, encourage him to delegate some of his work to you. Make it easy for him to do so.

Many managers complain that they cannot delegate. It is quicker and easier to do the job themselves. By the time they have overcome objections, explained what is needed, answered questions and finally checked that it has been done properly, it takes twice as much time to delegate as it would have taken to do the job themselves. Managers who can't or won't delegate don't get on. It is important for your future promotion that your boss should get on. You should therefore encourage your boss to delegate to you. Don't let him become so bogged down with work that he can't possibly be spared for promotion.

If this is the case his boss won't secure his promotion. Furthermore his boss may positively hold you and your colleagues back. He may take the view that your boss is tied down with routine because none of his staff are capable of accepting delegation. Also, the department run by an over-worked boss tends to creak a bit. People from creaking departments don't find it too easy to move sideways into another department, let alone move upwards.

If you want your boss to delegate to you, as you should, you must make it easy for him. Let him see that you regard the work he delegates to you as an opportunity, not an imposition. Try to avoid objections. Try to do the job, without continually going back to check up for further instructions. The first few jobs he delegates to you are likely to be simple ones. If you do them effectively and promptly, the boss may be encouraged to delegate more interesting jobs later.

You may argue that your own job gives you plenty of work without taking on the boss's job as well. However if you are going to get on, you have got to learn to organise yourself, to direct your staff effectively and to learn to delegate yourself. Hence one step in preparing to accept delegation from your boss is to get your own job thoroughly organised. The next step is to encourage your own subordinates to work effectively without constant supervision from you. Finally, start teaching one or more of them how to do parts of your own job. Indeed, if you can teach one of them to do your job completely, you are left free to accept extensive delegation from your own boss. You are also freely available for promotion, if someone is needed in a hurry.

There are other advantages to accepting delegation. The more he delegates to you, the less time he will spend getting in your way. It helps to prevent the problem of the boss actually doing part of your job by duplicating attendance at meetings and so on. However, the major benefit to you of accepting delegation is that you are starting to learn how to do the work of a more senior position. You are learning to do it in small instalments. You are training for promotion in the most positive way.

LEARN HIS JOB

There is no business situation more frustrating than this. Your boss is promoted, goes sick for a long period or dies. His department starts to malfunction because no one knows how to do his job. They may be potentially perfectly capable of doing it, but they don't know how. Senior management move in a new manager over your head. He rapidly digs himself in, partly on the basis of his experience and largely on the knowledge that you and your colleagues individually have of the work of the department. You have to work to establish someone else in the job, which you could have been promoted into. If only . . .

If only you had made it your business to learn your boss's job. This has to be done with care. You must not scare him into seeing you as a rival, waiting to stab him at the earliest convenient moment. Rather, get your own job in order, encourage him to delegate as much as possible to you and learn those bits. Try to get a picture of his job as a whole. If you really are helping him and shifting some of the load off his shoulders, he will probably be happy to discuss problems with you.

Key areas to understand are his budget and objectives. There is a lot of dogsbody work to be done in preparing budgets. As managers get higher up the pyramid they are pro-

144

vided with their own accountants to help them in this area. Lower down they have to do most of the work themselves with whatever help they can get from their own non-accountant staff. If you help your boss, prepare his estimates of next year's revenue and expenditure; you are bound to learn quite a lot about his objectives, targets, problems and opportunities.

It is highly desireable that your boss's manager and his colleagues should recognise you as somebody they can turn to when the boss is away. Someone who can produce accurate information and someone who can get things done in the department in the boss's absence. It is not necessary to obtain the title of deputy, but it is highly desireable that people should start to recognise you as the heir apparent if anything happens to the boss.

Never forget that your boss is the key man so far as your future is concerned. This does not mean that you must become a complete yes man. You can and sometimes should disagree with him, but be careful how you do it. Never do it in such a way as to show him up in public.

Your boss will put up with quite a lot from you if he thinks you are good at your job and can help him in his. Don't be afraid to flatter him. Most men are susceptible to flattery if it is done tactfully and not too obviously. The boss likes to think his people respect and look up to him. It need not take much effort to convince him that you do.

16

Pitfalls

In concentrating on your own job, the department you work in and your own boss, it is wise to remember the wider scene. If you work in a very small firm, you probably know everyone who works for the firm and have a pretty good picture of the firm and all its activities.

Those who work in larger organisations probably have a much less complete picture. Their knowledge of the firm is frequently limited to the department or branch in which they work. This is a pity. You should try to be aware of how your boss and your department fit into the larger organisation chart, which admittedly show only the formal links. It is important that you know this, but the informal links are just as important.

COMPANY POLITICS

Politics is about power and influence. Politics is not a matter restricted to local and central government. Politics and politicians are at work in any large organisation. Some people exercise power and influence. Others have a potential to exercise power and influence but appear not to. Yet others, normally the majority in any organisation, exercise neither power nor influence.

It is not always obvious who the powerful people in an organisation are. It is natural to assume that the power lies with the people at the top of the pyramid — the chairman, managing director and members of the board. It is not however necessarily so. A lot depends upon who really make the decisions that matter. For our purpose we may take a rather narrow view of which decisions matter. There are those concerning individual promotions, transfer and pay rises and in particular those which will affect you. You are also concerned about attitudes and relationships within the company which will affect your work and the way you do it.

You may take a simple view. If you can see a better way of doing something, you may think it is just a matter of persuading your boss and then getting on with it. Real life is not as simple as that. People may be obstructive and stop your plan point blank or they may just make sure it doesn't work by being unco-operative.

Although your boss may be the man who says that your pay should be increased and by how much and may also be the man who recommends your promotion, a number of other people will have an influence on the outcome. The way they exercise this influence may be impartial. It may depend on their view of you as an individual, or on their view of your boss. However, the way they use their influence may in practice be influenced by interdepartmental politics.

We have seen that people sometimes operate as a group. As the group leader moves from company to company or is promoted within a company, so the other members of the group follow him. If the leader is personally successful in getting on and bringing prosperity to the group following him, the group will gradually become larger. Some of his chief followers will gradually build up their own team. As Dean Swift wrote:

> 'So naturalists observe, a flea
> Has smaller fleas that on him prey;
> And these have smaller still to bite 'em,
> And so proceed ad infinitum.'

Information of any importance to this informal grouping moves around with it fairly quickly. Similar informal groups exist in firms which have grown by merger or acquisition. The former members of a particular company that has been absorbed continue to operate an informal network for information and mutual aid. In a merger, it is interesting to observe the realignments as old enemies form alliances in the face of a common enemy. Here and there someone defects to the enemy. He sees his opportunity not in closing ranks with his old colleagues but in trying to join the opposition and ingratiating himself by acting as a source of information.

This emphasises the point that you need to be extremely careful of company politics and even more careful if you think of joining the game yourself. Even where a company appears to have a ruling class or an inner circle where power resides, it does not follow that all its members pull together. However tight-knit the group, there may well be tension and rivalry. There will be those who are strengthening their position in the group and those who are about to drop off the edge. If you do feel the need to try to attach yourself to such a group, be careful not to attach yourself to the member who is being squeezed out. He will, more than likely, be the easiest to attach to because he feels the draught and is looking for potential allies.

Many managers take the view that they want nothing to do with company politics. However carefully they avoid personal involvement in any grouping, they are bound to be affected to some degree. Your plans and pet projects may be blocked, your key staff filched. You may even find your budget slashed or your area of operations drastically reduced as a result of the operation of company politics. The moral is try to keep yourself fully aware of company politics even if you do not want to play yourself.

One common area of politics is the strife between line management and staff. In many companies, line managers resent the power and cost of the central staff. Line managers feel that they are left with the real problems while the staff live in the luxury of an ivory tower headquarters. The staff for their part frequently regard line managers as quarrelsome

148

robber barons, slow to comprehend anything but their immediate self interest. On the whole, staff tend to be in the more vulnerable position. In times of financial stringency, senior managers have a marked inclination to cut non-productive staff first. When a company is taken over, the new owners need the line managers at least for the first few months. They rarely need all the headquarters staff.

For those with an eye to promotion, some time in a staff job in the company head office has its merits, not least that it provides an opportunity to familiarise yourself with the political setup. It also gives you a chance to study senior management at work. If you really want to get to the top, the best route probably lies through line management, where you have responsibility both for planning and for achievement of results. You can build a reputation as a manager who gets results.

LINKS WITH TOP MANAGEMENT

After that slight digression, let us come back to an area that offers you both opportunity and pitfall. On the face of it, links with senior management must be a good thing for anyone with aspirations to promotion. Senior management have the power and influence to select you for promotion, for key assignments and to look after your rewards.

This is certainly true in a family-controlled company, where the fastest route to the top may still be to marry the boss's daughter. In modern business conditions, it will not be sufficient just to marry her and sit back. You will also have to work at it, because powerful families have learnt the folly of handing over their power to the incompetent. So while marrying into the family who control a firm will probably result in a well paid job, it will only lead to the top if you show adequate ability and a willingness to work.

Being known to top management in any circumstances can't be a bad thing. It seems fair to assume this on the basis that any advertising is better than none. However, in a very

The fastest route to the top may still be to marry the boss's daughter

large company, knowing a top manager who is many levels removed from you may do you no good at all. The decisions about your pay and promotion are probably made at a level well below his and he may well cause antagonism and resistance if he intervenes in favour of one individual. He can of course suggest your name for a particular assignment, but may well be too remote to have any effect. If a senior man takes too obvious an interest in a very junior manager, it may even do him harm. It can annoy and antagonise his immediate boss. At worst, it can even lead to his being used as a pawn, when budgets are being cut and programmes reviewed.

There can, of course, be times when your job involves frequent contact with more senior people than yourself. This can be highly dangerous. In the course of the job you will probably have to make moves that will annoy managers senior to yourself. There may be no way out of this if you are to do your job properly. Your only protection lies in doing your job properly and achieving the objectives you have been set. Hopefully the senior man who has been responsible for your work will see that you are suitably placed on its completion. Don't bank on this.

Take the case of Bill Atkins. He was given responsibility with the Alpha Company for a large project — project 'X'. There was widespread disbelief both in the company and the outside world that the company could meet its project objectives. There were widespread accusations that the company had been given the project as a result of political lobbying. The Beta Corporation, a foreign company, was particularly bitter because they had already obtained a vague commitment and felt that they were entitled to the order. They continued to lobby the public body responsible for the project. By the time Bill Atkins was appointed one of the directors of Alpha Company, he had become firmly associated with the project and was publicly seen to be associated with it. It would do him no good if the project failed. Alpha were also saddled with two main subcontractors.

Bill Atkins got stuck in to the job. The customer attitude was pretty frigid and a high proportion of managers in his own company wanted nothing at all to do with the project. They thought it would fail. In due course Bill succeeded in improving the customer atmosphere. At the end of two years he also completed the first main stage of the project on time. This was recognised by a bonus of about 8 per cent of his annual salary.

At this stage the underlying position changed in an unsatisfactory way. The Alpha company's financial position was deteriorating. A new managing director was appointed. As luck would have it, he was headhunted from the Beta corporation. In due course a number of his cronies followed him over to Alpha. Amongst these was the man who had been responsible for project 'X' in the Beta Corporation, before they lost the order. He and another manager who had worked for him in Beta, both became directors of the Alpha company. Bill's project was finally brought to a finish, but did not meet the performance levels specified in the original tender. Bill had not been responsible for what went into the tender. He was assigned to the project only a few days before Alpha got the order. He had pointed out the probable performance shortfall — both verbally and in writing — from the time the possibility had first become clear to him in the early months of the project.

Things at this stage got really bad. The customer claimed compensation of over a million pounds for the performance shortfall, despite the fact that the project had been completed and was working very well. However, although it met all his real needs, the customer had a claim and intended to press it. Both the new managing director and the responsible director tried to negotiate their way out of it, failed miserably and merely succeeded in establishing a bad relationship with the customer, who was about to make decisions on where to place major fresh orders.

A hiatus was reached. Sales managers, who could see the possibility of losing the new orders, were very worried. The responsible director was subject to much criticism. The directors imported from Beta Corporation joined in a chorus of condemnation. Several managers, formally lying between Bill and the director in the company hierarchy, thought it must be possible to reach an agreement with the customer, but did not themselves want to get involved.

The director summoned Bill to his office to discuss the problem. Finally he said, in a very pointed fashion, 'Don't forget we're both on this raft together. Unless we can bring it in to land we've both had it.' Bill suggested that he should try to negotiate a settlement. Despite much disbelief, he finally succeeded in negotiating a settlement, which cost the Alpha company a quarter of a million pounds less than they were prepared to settle for. There was great relief all round. Bill, after a few weeks was given a bonus of £200 for his efforts. During the same year several sales managers, on the same basic rate of salary as Bill were rumoured to have taken home bonus payments of £4000. The director stepped safely off the raft, his position gradually became more secure and he prospered. He left Bill to fend for himself and he fared very badly in a series of non-jobs.

The moral of this tale is do not rely on your seniors in a business environment to look after you. Try to get your rewards set up in advance. By and large business pays you for what you are doing now or for services you will perform in the future. It very rarely bothers to pay for what is now completed unless it has previously entered into a firm agreement to do so.

It is pleasant to be on good terms with your colleagues at work. It is a mistake to believe that the pleasantries of business life have any meaning. In business, as in many other spheres, you get 'nowt for nowt and bloody little for sixpence'. Top managers may be very happy to use you either for the company's purposes or their own. Don't bank on their providing lasting benefits for you. You can make a success of the early stages of your career without ever meeting anyone from top management. It is sufficient to know and be known to your own boss and his boss. The larger the company for which you work, the truer this is.

CONSTRAINTS

In any organisation there are constraints on what you can do and upon what other people can do. In some companies any action which is both profitable and not clearly illegal is acceptable. Even in such companies, there may well be practical constraints. Such companies tend to be market-oriented. Anything likely to cause dissatisfaction among customers will be an effective constraint. If you have responsibility for certain objectives or for an area of activity, the need to keep the market happy is therefore a constraint on what you can do.

In practice, the constraints on your actions are more widespread than this. They arise generally because you can only get things done if other people, whose co-operation is needed, are co-operative or at least acquiescent. If they tend to be obstructive your task will be made difficult if not impossible. In considering any problem and its possible solutions, you need to bear in mind the constraints on your actions. From a promotion viewpoint it is of great importance to be aware of the constraints on your actions. Broadly, you will be judged on the extent to which you achieve your objectives. Mostly, you will not be set arbitrary objectives but will be involved in agreeing them. Once agreed, you will be expected to meet them.

If in agreeing your objectives you overlook the constraints on your actions, you may accept objectives which you cannot possibly meet. The constraints may be due to many factors. The market, government influence and the trade unions all impose constraints on a manager's freedom of action. These tend however to be felt at more senior levels of management. At the lower levels your boss's attitudes may be a constraint. Company politics and relationships between managers in your department and other departments may well be other constraints. For the junior manager, the extent of the office facilities or the availability of transport may be serious constraints. The company's rules may well be a bigger constraint for the junior manager than it is for the senior. They may severely limit the extent to which he can reward the people who work for him for accepting extra work and inconvenience. Management, like politics, deals with the art of the possible. You are concerned with the real world and not with an ideal one in which everyone behaves with exemplary reasonableness.

WAYS ROUND

Having identified the constraints, which limit the actions, open to you, appreciate that there are more ways than one of skinning a cat. Many people given an objective can see only one way of achieving it. Once they have seen a way to do it, they close their mind and go straight ahead, making a frontal attack on the problem. If there are constraints which make this in any way impossible, they are tempted to make this an excuse and say the job is impossible. This is a mistake. If you think carefully about it, there are generally several possible ways of achieving any objective.

If you identify the constraints that act as obstacles to your progress, you can find a way around them. If you make a proposal to your boss and he gives a flat 'No', don't argue with him. Don't even let it go and wait for the time when you can turn round and say 'I told you so'. Rather, withdraw carefully, trying to obliterate from his mind any trace of your proposal. Try to engage his mind quickly on some other subject. Later, try to make your proposal to him in some other more acceptable form. Perhaps you can make it part of a plan to meet some pet project of his. If you argue with him at his first rejection, you will merely help him to formulate his objections more clearly and set them in concrete.

In the last analysis, constraints are usually people and their attitudes. Try to avoid rows and arguments with people. They will produce the same result as confrontations with your boss — an impossible barrier. Much better to use persuasion and, with the really obdurate, try to outflank them by co-operation with someone else.

17

Increase Your Effectiveness

If you hope for promotion, one essential is to increase your effectiveness. You may resent this suggestion. You may argue that you are already very effective. You work hard and long and hold down a good job. Yes, but are you really effective?

Several years ago I felt tired and fed up. I was manager of a small department of about seventy people concerned with sales administration, factory liaison and allocation of output, technical information, market research and competitive intelligence, and the provision of an information service for professional firms concerned with our products.

I decided to carry out a survey of my activities over the period of a week. I made out sheets with the day of the week at the head of each column. The sheets were then divided horizontally into ¼ hour periods throughout the day. At the end of the week I studied the sheets and was horrified at what I found. I had taken a hurried pub lunch each day. This had averaged twenty minutes a day against the hour formally allowed for lunch each day. I had arrived early and left late every day. Over the five days I had worked some fifteen hours unpaid overtime and my briefcase was full of papers to read over the weekend. Yet, despite all this effort,

I had only kept pace with my intray. I could not honestly
look at my weeks work and say that I personally, had achieved
anything other than cope with day-to-day events. I had not
made any significant contribution to any decision. In effect
I had worked extremely hard but had very largely failed to
be effective. After careful consideration I came to the
conclusion that a large part of the problem arose because
of the way I used my time.

YOUR TIME

Your time is perhaps the most important resource you have.
It is also a finite resource. In other words, time will eventually
run out on you. As each minute goes by, it is gone forever.
If you have not used it properly, you cannot recall it. It is
gone forever. It pays you to find out how you use your time
and to ask yourself whether you are using it effectively.

It is pleasant sometimes to drift slowly and idly along in a
dinghy. It is enjoyable to spend hours in inconsequential
chatter with your spouse or potential spouse. These
activities have their own rewards and permit some recharging
of your mental and spiritual batteries. They have a part in a
full and enjoyable life. However, if you want to get on, you
need to take a more positive approach to your working time.

In order to use your time effectively you need first to
establish how you use it now. The best way may be, as I did,
to note how you use each quarter of an hour through the
week. Next consider your job in relation to the way you
used your time. What are your objectives? Did the way you
used your time enable you to make any progress towards
achieving those objectives?

If you have not previously thought about it, you will
probably find that, like me, you frittered away your time
on the day-to-day routine. You dealt with your correspondence, answered the 'phone, attended meetings, read reports
and had endless short discussions with your colleagues and
staff. Most if not all of your time is used up responding to
outside interference! You will be appalled at how little, if
any, time you have devoted to thinking about the managerial

aspects of your job, the underlying problems, policy, the future and the changing environment and problems you will have to meet, the development of your staff planning, devising ways to increase the effectiveness of your department. These are the real jobs. This is an awkward situation in which to find yourself. Finding the way out will be difficult. As an intrepid explorer once said 'When you're up to your arse in alligators, it is easy to overlook the reason you were trying to cross the swamp in the first place'.

If you find that this is an accurate diagnosis of your situation, what can you do about it? Well, you could take more work home or work longer hours. I believe that as a general rule this is a mistake. If you begin to work for too many hours, you become a bore. You lose close touch with your family. In time you become tired and lose even such effectiveness as you orginally had. If anything you should be cutting out the work you take home and reducing to a minimum the unpaid overtime you put in.

If you are to do this without reducing your effectiveness, you must examine your working day and try to reorganise it. The first essential is to recognise the need to organise your day so that you can devote significant chunks of it to the real job. The real job involves solid thinking. It cannot be squeezed into the odd five minutes between interruptions. You need time in decent undisturbed chunks. Ideally you need to be able to devote at least three-quarters of an hour at a time to your real problems. Many of them will be better planned if you devote a half day or even a whole day at a time to them.

You may think that this is wishful thinking. I assure you it is not. The first principle is to cut out unnecessary work. For each piece of work you do, ask yourself is it necessary to do it? If it is necessary, do you have to do it or could someone else do it?

Is it necessary for you to go to every meeting you do go to? What do you contribute to the work of the meeting? Is it really necessary for you to go or even be represented?

Do you read everything that drops into your intray? Particularly in the case of reports, minutes and papers of all sorts, you should ask yourself why you get it and what you will do as a result of reading it. A regular monthly report may come to you because one of your predecessors asked for a copy years ago. Circulation lists have a habit of becoming set in concrete. To have your name on certain circulation lists becomes almost a status symbol. If you don't need it, have your name cut off the circulation list.

Apart from anything else, this has the advantage that, if you have to do something arising from such a report on some occasion in the future, the originator will have to make a separate approach. In the meantime you will save the time taken to read that report every month.

If you have people working for you, perhaps some of the things that reach your intray could go direct to your subordinates. Perhaps they could deal with the matter entirely without reference to you. In some cases perhaps you can skim through a letter or report and pass it on to one of your people with a note saying what action you want them to take.

Even after making these improvements, you may find you still have a lot of reading to do. Try grading the material to be read. I still receive a lot of technical information, notes and commercial instructions. I do not need to read them meticulously from start to finish. I look at the subject covered and if it is of no interest at all, it goes straight into the out tray. If it is possibly of interest I read the introductory paragraphs and skim through the rest of the document effectively reading the subtitles and very little else. In this way a document, which might take ten or twenty minutes to read and understand, can be disposed of in a minute or so. This is a useful technique but start using it carefully, otherwise you may skim something which should have been carefully studied.

A great waster of time is the constant changing of priorities. Many years ago I was put in charge of a small cartographic drawing office. I was told that it was the bottleneck in our map production business. The technical controller's office was full of work waiting to come to us. The printing section was operating inefficiently because we could not get enough work to them. The outfit as a whole was continually failing to get its maps out on time.

After a few days I realised two things. First the drawing office was not the real bottleneck, only the scapegoat. Secondly the extent to which the drawing office had become a bottleneck arose because of constantly changing priorities. An examination of the job cards showed many ludicrous cases. The work to be done to update a map sheet was estimated at five days; work done to date six days; work outstanding, four days. This was not due to bad initial estimating.

A draughtsman would come in the morning and be given the sheet. He would study the sheet and the amendment material and get down to work. By mid-day a message would have arrived from the technical controller altering the priorities. The draughtsman would put away this job and be given another. Next day or a week later someone else would be given this job and start on it from the beginning.

This was not only wasteful of time but made the draughtsman cynical and demoralised. I decided to turn a blind eye to the instructions about changes or priority. If any job involved five man-days or less of effort, it was allocated to a draughtsman. Once started on it, he carried on and finished the job regardless. Within a month, by this simple measure, the position was transformed. Morale and hence output of the draughtsmen improved. The backlog of jobs was significantly reduced. Pressure on the section was reduced and all work could be approached in a more planned fashion. It became obvious that serious bottlenecks existed elsewhere in the map production process.

Indeed within a few more weeks we had the position so well under control that the draughtsmen were worrying about whether we had become so productive that some of them would lose their jobs. The point is that constantly changing priorities and butterflying from one task to another can be very harmful to your output. Try to concentrate the efforts of the people who work for you and avoid unnecessarily changing the priorities of their work.

In your own case try to concentrate your work so that you can deal with each bit relatively undisturbed. If you have a secretary, try to organise your day so that she can keep away phone calls and stray visitors for at least one period of an hour or so each morning and afternoon. This is a technique to be used with care. I recently 'phoned X, a manager in a firm with which I have done business for several years. I have dealt with X for several years. The conversation went like this:-

'X's secretary speaking.'

'Tom Watling here. Can I speak to X.'

'Who are you?'

'Tom Watling. I'm . . . . X knows me.'

'What do you want?'

By this time I'm getting a little irritated.

'To speak to X.'

'I'm sorry. X is at a meeting, can we 'phone you back?'

To cap it all, X never did ring back. So by all means use your secretary to protect you from continuous interruptions, but be careful how she does it. If she cannot do it tactfully, you will be better advised to find some other way of saving time — or get a more competent secretary.

One method I use both to save time and to make sure I use my time more effectively is to keep action lists. At least once a week, I sit down quietly for a quarter of an hour and list out all the things I know I ought to do. The lists take various forms. They contain actions, against which there are deadline dates. They also contain some long-term actions, which may take several weeks or months to complete, though in such cases I try to split them down into a number of discrete actions. Thirdly, there is usually a long list of minor actions, which will only take a few minutes to do. To every action on the three lists I allot a priority and I try to take action in priority order. However if I have only five minutes available I chose an item from list 3 instead of list 1 or 2. I also attack list 3 if a visitor does not arrive on time for an appointment. On days when I feel that I don't want to work and can't concentrate, I warm up with half an hour or so working down list 3. As the week goes by new items are added to the lists. At the end of the week I review progress and make out fresh lists for the coming week.

When you have staff working for you it is useful also to keep lists of what they are supposed to do, with the date by which it is to be done. Some ineffective managers become a laughing stock with their staff and colleagues. They continually ask for certain things to be done but never notice whether they have been done or not. This may be due to forgetfulness or to the feeling that to check up shows a lack of confidence in the people. You want to avoid this. You also want to avoid going to the opposite extreme of constantly checking up in a nagging fashion. Keeping the action lists should not only make you more effective but hopefully will also make those that work for you more effective too. A reputation as 'the manager, who never forgets', can be useful.

DO YOUR HOMEWORK

I do not suggest that you should take a briefcase full of papers home every night. Rather the reverse. So far as possible I believe in leaving work behind when I go home. What I do suggest is that you should be careful and thorough in your preparation.

This is particularly so with meetings of all sorts. Most people realise that if they are going to address a meeting of 100 people that some preparation will be necessary. It is equally important to prepare all your business meetings. If you go to see your boss or arrange to meet a colleague, you should have done your homework beforehand.

First you should know why you are going to the meeting. Even if it is a regular weekly routine meeting, you must have some reason for going. If it is just habit, see if it can be dropped. Assuming there is a reason, what do you intend to achieve at the meeting? This may be something clear cut, like getting agreement to spend a certain amount of money or permission to take on additional staff. It may be less precisely defined. For instance you may visit a colleague to tell him about a project and how it is expected to develop. You may do this as a precaution in order to head off possible opposition from him in the future.

Whatever the objective of the meeting have it clear in your head. Then plan the meeting. If there is any past history make sure you are aware of it. Take a look through the recent correspondence, if any. If the meeting is with someone outside your own department, check up on whether there are any outstanding disputes or problems between your department and his. If you are meeting a customer of your firm, make sure you speak to the salesman first; find out what the customer buys from you; if you are a capital goods manuafcture, find out what equipment of yours he has installed. Find out from the salesmen what the customer has on order and whether there are any problems on the account.

You may think it unlikely that anyone outside sales the service organisation of your company would visit a customer. This is not always so. Your firm may well buy goods or services from your own customers. You may engage in some joint enterprise or project. You may even belong to the same organisation, which lobbies for common objectives.

I find it useful to keep a hardbacked notebook, in which I keep a handwritten note about all the business meetings I attend. I take the book with me and during the meeting note down the date and names of those present. I also note down any decisions made, any significant items of information and any promises of future information or action. Sometimes it is inappropriate to take notes at the meeting. In such, fairly rare, cases I make a note as soon as I can after the meeting.

I use the same notebook to keep a note of key items of information, decisions and promises that arise from conversations including telephone conversations. I make particular point of recording anything which I undertake to do myself and mark it clearly in the margin. I cancel the mark, when I complete the action. This gives me an easy method of checking on my outstanding actions, arising from meetings and conversations. It also provides a useful aid to preparing for meetings.

Some managers also find it useful to keep a personal note-book about people they meet. This must obviously be kept more discreetly and is probably best kept at home. If you deal with a lot of people at work, you may find it difficult to retain in your mind all the minor personal things they mention to you. If you meet a representative of another firm after an interval of a year, it is useful to have an aide-memoire about him. For any salesman or sales manager whose memory for such details is poor, such a notebook is essential. Into it go notes of what people tell you of their family, their hobbies, their holidays, their investments or any other aspects that they have expanded on in conversation. Train journeys and business lunches in particular bring forth such confidences. If next time you meet, you are able by some question or comment to show that you remember what they have told you about themselves and their family, it is likely to pay of in a better and closer relationship.

A very successful sales manager I once knew carried this idea to great lengths. He met literally hundreds of senior managers of customers firms each year, but rarely met them more than once or twice a year. He kept a card index with a card for every contact, complete with a photograph for almost all of them. He was not amused when I asked him where he kept the fingerprints. His system was extremely effective. The photographs were not as difficult to obtain as you might imagine. Many of them were taken from the trade press or the customers' house journal. Where this was not possible, he frequently managed to take a photograph himself of the customer standing beside a piece of equipment or visiting the sales managers office. This sales manager was never caught out by failing to recognise his contacts when he called on them. Nor was he ever at a loss for small talk to warm the opening of a meeting or to keep a business lunch going.

The real point is, whoever you are going to meet, go prepared. Know what you want to achieve from the meeting and don't allow yourself to be tripped up because you have failed to make a thorough preparation for the meeting. The more you know about the individuals you are going to meet, the more effective the meeting is likely to be.

MORE EFFECTIVE WORK – NOT MORE WORK

I am often told by colleagues how hard they work. Some people take pride in the fact that they work late every night and take work home with them at the weekend. They are proud of the fact and expect to be applauded for their devotion. It is noticeable that such people are often not very prod-

*Some wives are so unwelcoming that their
husbands feel happier at work*

uctive. Their efficiency begins to drop as a result of long hours.
They become tired and irritable. Their irritability upsets the
people they deal with and the whole business becomes a
vicious circle. It is, of course, true that some wives are so unwelcoming that their husbands feel happier at work. Less
cynically some managers work during the week away from
home — in effect weekend commuting. Such managers may
think that they may as well work during the evenings rather
than sit in their digs. This has an unfortunate effect on their
subordinates, who begin to feel guilty if they are not available
in the evening when their boss wants them. The old proverb
'All work and no play, makes Jack a dull boy' contains a lot
of truth.

There will of course, be times when you do have to work
long hours to deal with a particularly difficult situation; to
deal with a sudden crisis; or to meet a deadline. On the whole,
I believe it is a mistake to work long hours regularly. The secret
is not to work longer hours, but to work more effectively. This
is largely a matter of using your time effectively as we have

seen. The real answer is not to work more but to work smarter.

Leslie Thomas in his novel *Tropic of Ruislip* quotes the inscription on a Watford tombstone:

"The wonder of the world, the beauty and the power,
the shape of things, their colours, lights and shades; these
I saw. Look ye also while life lasts.'

That seems to me good advice to any manager. It is important to do you job well and to plan your promotion, but it is not the whole of life. Work smarter and enjoy your leisure.

LOOK BELOW THE SURFACE

If you want to be effective, learn not to take things at face value. It is nice to think that everything in business life works in a logical businesslike way. Everyone works to the best of their ability to maximise the profits of their firm. Each individual co-operates with his colleagues for the common good. It is nice to believe this. It may be wiser to retain a healthy scepticism. Always keep your eye out for the hidden motive.

The hard fact of life is that in most situations people act for their own motives. They put forward apparently rational ideas, suggestions or objections. The real reason may well be that they think that if the idea is adopted, it will save them work. They may be afraid that their prospects or even their job is threatened. Whatever idea is being aired, the motives behind people's reactions are likely to be mixed.

Two very strong motives are greed and fear. Neither should be appealed to openly. However if you have to get a proposal agreed by any individual or group, it is likely to be helpful if the proposal can contain some benefit, however small, for them. Fear is a very strong motive and you should be careful not to start it working against you. People are easily frightened. They believe any change may be against their interest and fear it. This is why it is so important always to consult people, who may be affected by any plan of yours, as early as possible

If practicable, any plan or new project should be discussed stage by stage with all those affected. They should be given the chance to feed in their own ideas and suggestions. If carefully done, they will accept the plan or project as their own and you will have completely disarmed the fear, which could otherwise work so strongly against you.

If you want to be effective, you must consider what other people want, not just what you think is best. You must look under the surface to find out the 'reasons why'. If you can do this you are well on the way to managing people; both people who formally work for you and those who don't. You will be well on the way to making youself more effective.

MAKING MISTAKES

You can go through life, making very few mistakes. Some people seem scared of ever making a mistake. Indeed some people believe that if they make mistakes, this will be held against them for ever and will hold back their promotion. It may even be true that in some occupations, such as the Civil Service, the mistakes you make are noted on your record and held against you for some considerable period. Because of this fear of mistakes, some people go through life with extreme caution. In assessing situations, they tend to overemphasise the risks. They are more concerned to be seen not to be at fault, than they are to succeed. They concentrate on 'keeping their nose clean'. They are umbrella men — whatever happens they are always covered.

Don't be afraid of making some mistakes. You must be prepared to back your own judgement. Inevitably your judgement will sometimes be wrong. That doesn't really matter as long as you learn from your mistakes. Anyone can make a mistake once, only a fool makes the same mistake twice. The man who never makes a mistake misses a lot of opportunities.

I am not suggesting that you should take reckless risks. What I am suggesting is that once you have considered a situation you will be faced with a number of alternative courses of action. One may be dead safe, riskless and probably pretty unprofitable. The course of action which seems to offer the best balance of risk and profit, will rarely if ever be completely free of risk. Successful people try to minimise their risks, but they do not completely avoid them.

It is best to overcome fear of mistakes early in your career.

167

At that stage your bosses expect that you will make some mistakes. If you do find yourself restrained by the fear of making mistakes, ask yourself, what is the worst that can happen to you if you do make a mistake. In most civilised countries the worst that can happen is that you are sacked. You won't be shot, just fired. If that happens, you go out and get another job or set yourself up in your own business.

In this respect Americans seem less inhibited than Britons. In the United Kingdom, people are becoming more used to changing jobs frequently. But people in large companies, in the nationalised industries, in local and central government, still largely look on their job as one that will last until they reach retirement age. If you want to get on, you must shake off the belief that you must marry the company you work for . . . till retirement doth you part.

Be prepared to make mistakes. Probably the worst will not happen. If you make a few mistakes and learn from them you may well find that you get on faster. To grow up and enter adult life, you had to cut loose from your mother's apron strings. In the same way to become effective in the business world, you must learn to make your own decisions. You'll never get anywhere, if you always have to ask the boss — just in case.

John Brown was a very pleasant, hardworking man. After twenty years service with a company, he had risen to be deputy to the manager of the sales office. The popular story about him was that one of the reps looked into the office one morning and said to him: 'Nice day, Mr Brown, isn't it?'. 'Just a minute, I'll check with the boss', came the reply.

If you are to get on, you must learn to stand firmly on your own feet. The more effective you become, the easier this will be. The key is learning how to use your time effectively. Having done this, make sure that you do your homework. You can do it perfectly effectively in the office, there's no need to take it home with you. Look below the surface. It is surprising how many people profess the highest motives while actually being guided by the most primitive self-interest. Don't be over-conscious of risks — you'll rarely get the chance to bet on an absolute certainty.

Above all, remember you don't need to work more — just smarter.

18

Improve Your Basic Skills

Some people accumulate all their knowledge and experience by the age of twenty and coast on this stock for the rest of their life. There are some people who believe their education is complete when they leave school, graduate or qualify in their profession. The man who gets on never stops learning. Part of the business of becoming more effective lies in improving your own basic skills. Not only does this help you towards promotion, it may also help you to enjoy life more.

If you are to become more effective, it is of course important to keep up to date with developments. This can be done by reading the professional trade and specialist papers. You should also read the latest books on your speciality. You may of course have just started at the bottom, as a clerk in an office, and think that this advice does not apply to you. You couldn't be more wrong. You can read about modern office techniques. More important, perhaps, you can start to read about the trade in which your company operates. You can also start reading about management so that you are prepared when the opportunity appears.

READING AND REMEMBERING

Reading is perhaps one of the most basic skills we use. It is one of the three R's taught in the most primitive of schools.

Yet it is also one of the most important. I have suggested above that you should increase your regular reading. In an earlier chapter I emphasised the need to use your time effectively. You may feel that if you are to economise in the use of your time that you need to cut down on your reading, not increase it.

There is one way out of the dilemma. Learn to read more quickly. Most of us read quite slowly — at a rate of about 250 words a minute. If you read at a rate of somewhere between 200 and 300 words a minute, you should be able to at least double this rate. What is more important you should be able to achieve better comprehension of the material you have read at the faster rate.

One way of learning to read faster is to persuade your company to send you on a faster reading course. An alternative is to teach yourself to read faster with the help of one of the many books on the subject. There are at least two, available at the time of writing, in paperback for less than £1; *Read Better, Read Faster* by Manya and Eric De Leeuw (published by Pelican) and *Speed Reading* by Tony Buzan (published by Sphere Books). Learning to read faster and more effectively will require quite a small investment of money. However a considerable investment of time and effort will be needed.

Reading is of importance to the man on his way up. Perhaps memory is of even greater importance. It is important to be able to remember at least the main argument and key facts from the papers you read. There are occasions when you meet and talk to people that you cannot pull out your notebook to record what is said. In such circumstances, you may be given information, which it is important to remember at least until you can write it down. It can be embarrassing if you forget names and faces. It can be irritating if you forget telephone numbers, addresses and other basic facts.

If you have a poor memory, it will not improve on its own. It requires some effort. Most people find it comparatively easy to remember things which interest them. Perhaps the secret is that when they are interested they concentrate their attention. Perhaps also, if they have learnt something that interests them, they may go back to it in their mind later in the day. This helps to strengthen the memory.

If your memory is poor, you should ce~
prove it as part of your plan for promotion
are courses in memory training. I went on o
ago and enjoyed it. There are a number of bo
helping you to improve your memory. One o~
back is *Speed Memory* by Tony Buzan (publish
Books).

TALKING

If reading and memory are basic skills for the man who is
planning for promotion, talking is even more basic. Talking
is one of the two basic ways we communicate our ideas to
other people. We talk to people as individuals or in small
groups. We talk on the telephone and we talk in public.

Our boss and most other people we meet make quite
important judgements about us. Such judgements are greatly
influenced by the way we speak. If you have never heard
yourself speak, it is well worth borrowing a tape recorder and
speaking into it. Try talking as you expect to, next time you
go to see your boss. Then play it back to yourself. You may
be surprised at the result, but don't let it put you off. Notice
the things about your speech which put you off. Is it clear and
easy to understand? Or is it slurred and unclear? Is it very loud
or soft? Is it harsh? Is it staccato, like a sergeant major? Do
you repeat yourself? Is your speech full of 'ah's', 'um's', 'you
know's' and 'sort of's'? Do you speak too fast, too slow or
just right?

The first time I heard my voice on a tape recorder, I was
amazed. You may be too. With time and care you can probably
improve your normal speech. You will also probably find that
you can make an improvement by planning the main points
you intend to make. In any conversation it is worth remembering that talking is only part of it. Listening to the other party
is at least as important. If you are too busy thinking what you
are going to say next, you may miss what the other party is
saying.

It is all too easy to switch off while someone drones on. In
business it can be dangerous, particularly if it is your boss who

Try to concentrate on what he has to say. At the
the learn a lesson yourself. If you are going to retain
interest of people you talk to, keep your comments short
and to the point. If you want to drive home a point, don't
just repeat it. Say it in different words and try to add an
example or anecdote to help drive it home.

Speaking on the 'phone is much the same as talking to someone face to face. Remember though, that he does not see your
face or gestures. It is particularly important to speak clearly
and sufficiently clearly for the other party to comprehend
what you say.

PUBLIC SPEAKING

As you progress up an organisation, it is more likely that you
will sometimes have to speak in public. This may take the form
of a presentation of a report or proposal to a large group. It
may be a lecture to a group of trainees. It may be a short
presentation speech to someone leaving the firm or getting
married. It may be an after-dinner speech or it may be a speech
to a public meeting.

The higher up the hierarchy you go, the less easy it is to
avoid such occasions. I have had to speak in public a great many
times. Twice it was absolute disaster. The first time was when I
worked for the Ordnance Survey of Great Britain. I was detailed to go and speak to a Round Table meeting one evening.
I had never spoken in public before. I made no proper preparation. I stood up and talked, eventually getting into an endless
catalogue of the various kinds and scales of map we produced.
The audience were bored stiff. My only consolation was that
the supper was lousy and I wasn't paid for talking to them.

However I determined to learn from the experience and the
next time I had to make a speech of this sort, I prepared more
carefully. I made a selection of what aspects of the work I
would talk about. I made some notes on a card to keep me
on the right track. I also took some slides and other items to
act as props. In the result I made a passable speech, which
restored my confidence and brought a very pleasant letter of
thanks to my boss. If I may point a moral from my own

experience, I had made a complete ass of myself on the first occasion. I learnt from my mistakes and took the earliest opportunity to have another — and more effective — go.

The second disaster many years later was when I allowed myself to be persuaded to give a public lecture in London organised by a Junior Chamber of Commerce. The speaker before me was applauded. I then read out my carefully prepared speech. When I finished, stoney silence. It was not the material that was wrong. That has subsequently been successfully used in a book and also for an article. The mistake was to read the speech. The fact that I was nervous at addressing an audience of 200 and that I had never previously spoken to a group larger than 40 was no excuse. When you read a speech, it just does not come over naturally or spontaneously. It is far better, after you have thoroughly prepared your speech, to reduce it to a few headings on a card or series of cards. Providing you have done your preparation carefully and know your subject, you can give a good natural spontaneous speech based on your notes.

Preparing a speech to be given in public is, I find, a very laborious and time-consuming process. If I am going to speak for half an hour it can take me up to ten hours to prepare my speech, not to mention time spent on devising and producing visual aids. You are well advised to get some practice early in your career. However, it is sensible to learn something about it before committing yourself too far. Some large companies regard the ability to speak competently in public as so important that they run short courses for their own staff. It is also possible to go on more generally available courses.

There are books which tell you how to speak in public and reading one of these is certainly better than nothing. I believe there is a lot to be gained from going on a course, if you can. The opportunity to practice in front of a friendly but critical class of fellow students can be extremely helpful. If you cannot persuade your firm to send you on such a course, I believe some local authorities include public speaking among their adult education classes.

NEGOTIATING

Negotiating is a special form of talking. As a general rule, the more senior you become in an organisation, the more you become involved in negotiation. You may negotiate special sales terms with a customer, a loan from the bank; a settlement with a trade union or special support from a government department or agency. An important part of the work of many senior managers is negotiation. Like so many other managerial activities, it is not primarily a matter of special qualifications or powers.

Negotiation is another skill which you should take every opportunity to develop. The key factor in successful negotiation is preparation. It is essential to do your homework before each negotiating meeting. You need to see quite clearly your own objectives and the limits on your authority to conclude the negotiation. It is obviously easier to negotiate if you have some room for manoeuvre. Perhaps, less obviously, you should know the extent of the powers of the person with whom you are negotiating. You should also try to build up a picture of what he wants out of the negotiation.

It is a mistake to see the person with whom you are negotiating as an enemy. It is equally mistaken to look for victory in negotiation. The essence of a successful negotiation is that both parties come out of the process satisfied. They should both feel that they have obtained a beneficial deal and one that is fair. If the other party ends the negotiation by accepting a deal which he feels is unfair and not in his best interests, then you will have laid the foundation stone for future trouble. An excellent book on the subject has been written by K.H. Nothdurft. It is called *The Complete Guide to Successful Business Negotiation* (published by Leviathan House). It is worth reading.

WRITING

Apart from talking, writing is the most important method of business communication. Another of the basic three R's, it is an essential skill for the man who seeks promotion. It is not necessary to develop a great literary style. What is necessary is to write simply and clearly. Whatever you write should be understandable at a first read. It should be completely un-ambiguous and free from padding.

The only way to improve your writing is to practise it. One of the best guides is *The Complete Plain Words* originally written by Sir Ernest Gowers and later revised by Sir Bruce Fraser. It is published by HMSO and at the time of writing costs £1. This book was first written to try to improve the standard of written English in the Civil Service. Whether it succeeded in its object, I do not know, but it is certainly a great help to anyone who wants to write more clearly and effectively.

In writing anything it is important to put yourself in the place of the recipient. Try to read your letter or report with his eyes. Does it tell him what he wants to know? Will it be clear to him or is there any possibility that he will fail to understand it? If there is any doubt in your mind it is probably worth rewording it.

Try to write as clearly as you can so that you transfer your thoughts as simply and clearly as you can from your mind to the mind of your reader. However, do keep a sense of propor-tion. Do not spend hours over a once-off routine memo. Do not always aim for perfection in your writing.

Remember Mr Jones, the senior manager, who was so concerned about the grammar and literary value of his monthly report. Be concerned about the message. As long as that comes over clearly to the recipient that is the main consideration. It is worth remembering that what you say is soon forgotten, whereas what you write will be seen each time the file is turned up. A real howler in writing will take a long time to live down.

On the same tack, if you are going to be rude to someone, it is better to be rude in person to his face or even on the 'phone. If you commit your rudeness to paper, it will linger for a long time and make for continued bad blood — and possibly a long and increasingly acrimonious correspondence between you and the recipient. By contrast you can express yourself much more freely and forcefully in talking to some-one. You can have a real bust up and be on friendly terms again once the tension has been released; but not if it has been committed to writing.

MAKING A CASE

A special aspect of writing is making a case. Occasionally you will have to make a written case; perhaps a justification of a new project or for some change you plan; perhaps you want a new machine or a bigger budget next year.

To make such a case you need to be quite clear about your objective. If you are seeking a decision, be clear on who can make the decision. It may not be your boss, though the case will have to be submitted through him. Whoever it is, have him clearly in your mind as you write your case. Try to make the case in a logical sequence. State the problem you are trying to solve or the opportunity you aim to exploit. Give some brief background information if that is necessary to understanding the proposal. If your proposal is a major one it will be necessary next to examine all the factors affecting the problem and its solution. Set out the various possible solutions. There is very rarely only one possible way to exploit an opportunity or solve a problem. The real possibilities should be set down. Against each give the advantages and disadvantages that would arise from adopting that solution. Finally give your proposed solution with the reasons for its adoption. Expand this solution into an outline plan of action.

Such a case will inevitably run to several pages. Put yourself in the place of the decision-maker. Is he someone who will expect the full case or does he prefer a succinct statement of the bare essentials? If he does it may be wise to provide him with just a brief statement of the opportunity or problem, your proposed plan and the benefits which will arise from adopting your plan. If your proposal has to go through several levels before it reaches the decision maker, it may be better to provide such a brief statement as a management summary and back it with the full case.

Remember that however much you polish your writing skills, the typing pool or your secretary can make a nonsense of it. Unless you have reached a position near the top, with a top class executive secretary, it will pay you to read important outgoing papers before you sign them. Mistakes do get made. Whole lines can be left out and reduce a well thought out statement to nonsense.

In this chapter I have given a rough canter through the basic skills, that you need if you are to travel far up the pyramid. It is easy to mention them. It will take you time and trouble to develop these skills. They are however basic. You can develop them for yourself even if your present firm doesn't want to know. They are skills that will be of value to you if you move to another company. Indeed, they are skills which you will find useful even if you decide to change not just companies but occupation as well.

19

Business Meetings

Meetings are an important part of modern life. Most large organisations are pyramid-shaped. However, they do not operate on the simple military principle of orders being handed down from the top. Most large business and governmental organisations operate on the basis of decisions which arise out of discussions and consultation. The main vehicle for such discussion is the meeting.

As part of your plan for promotion you must equip yourself both to take part in meetings and to organise them. Meetings may take several forms. Basically they are either formal meetings or informal. Formal meetings are arranged with a chairman to conduct the meeting, an agenda and with minutes to record the outcome. Informal meetings are less structured but are probably much more frequent. Meetings of either sort should not just happen. They should take place for a purpose. That may seem obvious but it is surprising how many meetings appear to take place for little purpose.

Although informal meetings are more frequent and possibly more important, I will discuss formal meetings first. Much that applies in the case of formal meetings you can apply equally to informal meetings.

Formal meetings give you the opportunity to meet a range

of managers other than your own boss. They give you the chance to meet colleagues and seniors in other departments as well as occasionally meeting much more senior members of your own line management. Making your mark by a competent performance at formal meetings may be your first chance to make a good impression on others beyond your boss. In a sense the business meeting is the manager's stage. Don't muff your performances.

PREPARATION

Going to a meeting is not just a matter of rushing out of your office and into the meeting. To be effective, you need to prepare before you go to any meeting. In terms of your own promotion plan, it is worth remembering that meetings provide a shop window in which you can display your merits. This does not mean that meetings are an occasion for you to show off or hog the limelight. Rather the reverse.

The first thing to do is to find out what the meeting is about. This involves reading the letter or memo, setting up the meeting; reading the agenda and any other papers that may have been circulated, and reading the minutes of any previous meetings on the subject. Having read these papers you should ask yourself why you are going to the meeting?

If the answer is not clear to you, it is advisable to have a word on the 'phone with the person who has called the meeting. Discuss the matter with him and try to establish what contribution you will be able to make. Note, however, that directors and senior managers sometimes call meetings of their own staff in order to address them or exhort them on some subject. If the meeting is of that sort, your director will not appreciate your 'phoning up to discuss whether or not you should go.

As part of the question 'Why am I going?', ask whether you are going on your own account or to represent your boss, your company or some association. If you are going in a representative capacity you need to do more homework before you go. If you represent your boss, you should have a discussion with him. Make sure that you know his views on the various matters on the agenda. Discuss the limits on how far you can commit him in terms of work or decisions. Find out if there are any particular results he wants from the meeting.

If you are going to represent your company at an outside meeting it is even more important to prepare. You should discuss the points on the agenda with the various company experts. You should be quite clear as to the extent to which you can commit the company and the sort of point which you will have to refer back.

You will of course make the simple routine checks on the time and place of the meeting and work out how to get there on time. As part of your preparation it is sensible to check on who else will be at the meeting and to think out in advance what their attitudes are likely to be. Finally, you should think out how you intend to put over the points you have to make and plan how you will achieve your objectives at the meeting.

ATTENDING

It is both courteous and sensible to arrive at any meeting a few minutes before it is due to start. You will of course take all the relevant papers with you. It can create a very bad impression if you fail to bring a paper containing information to which it is vital that you refer. If for any reason you cannot get to the meeting, let the person calling the meeting know, as early as possible, that you can't get there. If possible arrange for someone to go in your place.

Pay attention to what is being said, even on agenda points of no direct significance to you. It is always wise to keep your own notes of what is said. Some people take a long time to bring out minutes of meetings. You may well want to brief other people in your department about the meeting and start taking action on the decisions immediately without waiting for the minutes to arrive.

In making your contributions, be short and keep to the point. Until you have plenty of experience avoid trying to make jokes or facetious comments. They may not be understood Trying to explain them can be both difficult and embarrassing. Avoid being drawn into discussion with those sitting next to you when someone else is talking to the meeting. A good chairman will not allow you to. You should avoid taking advantage of a weak chairman; it reduces the effectiveness of the meeting.

If there is opposition to your ideas or proposals, try to deal with the people concerned in a rational way. Explain your point, try to understand their point of view. Above all try to get them on your side and try to avoid forcing them into an entrenched position of rigid opposition. Once people have taken up a formal position of opposition in public, it can be very difficult to change their attitude. It may often be wise to postpone a decision to a future meeting if opposition is building up. This gives you an opportunity to lobby the opposition and try to make some converts outside the meeting.

If you have gone to the meeting to represent your boss make sure you report to him on any points of importance arising at the meeting. If any of them are of importance to your colleagues, they should be told as well. The best way of doing this is probably by writing an internal memo.

SECRETARY

At some stage you may be asked to act as secretary to a meeting. If may well be a meeting that your work requires you to hold but your boss wants to chair. There is no great procedure for acting as secretary to a normal working meeting. There are however certain points you should attend to if the meeting is to go successfully.

The first thing is to have a brief discussion with the chairman to discuss the purpose of the meeting and the arrangements to be made. You need to agree with him:

1   Who is to be invited to the meeting.
2   The main agenda points.
3   The time and place of the meeting.

Once this is agreed, the next step is to 'phone around the key people whose attendance is necessary at the meeting. Check that the proposed time and place are convenient for them. If you have a secretary, this is the sort of job she should do for you. If you need a conference room for the meeting, then this should be booked as soon as possible.

After this a note should be sent to everyone invited to the

meeting. This will tell them the purpose of the meeting, the time and place, the agenda and any special administrative arrangements. For instance if people are coming from other parts of the country, you will need to tell them about any special car parking arrangements. If they have not previously been to your office, you will need to provide directions for getting there.

For the day of the meeting there are a number of minor administrative tasks to be done. Once again if you have a secretary she will do them for you, otherwise you will be lumbered with them. Check that there are enough chairs in the meeting room and that any necessary equipment, e.g. flipchart board, is in the room. For a meeting of any size — or a meeting with people from outside, provide pencil and paper for each person attending. Make sure that there are ash-trays and arrange for tea or coffee to be brought into the meeting.

Arrive at the meeting in good time yourself and bring a few spare copies of the agenda and papers in case anyone has failed to bring their own copy. As people arrive note the fact and make sure you know who everyone is. If there are a lot of strangers to you, it is a wise precaution to provide a signing in sheet. Ask people to fill in their name in block capitals and to give their address/phone number. This is particularly necessary if it is a large meeting with people coming from a number of different companies or organisations.

At the meeting itself, sit next to the chairman, so that you can prompt him if he overlooks a point. Avoid fussing over him like an old hen, it will both make him look ridiculous and irritate him. Take full and careful notes throughout the meeting, so that you will have an aide-memoire on which to base your minutes of the meeting. After the meeting, check up to see that no confidential papers have been left in the conference room.

After the meeting, comes the secretary's most important task, the preparation of the minutes. If possible these should be written up on the day of the meeting or at the latest on the next working day. If you leave it any longer, you will find that some points have escaped you. Minutes that arrive a couple of days after a meeting can be very useful. Those that do not arrive until a day or two before the next meeting on the same subject are not very helpful and are a public indication of inefficiency.

The minutes themselves, should be as brief as possible. You should avoid the trap of recording what everyone said. All that is needed is a record of the decisions and of any key information given to the meeting, which influenced these decisions. Where it was agreed that some action should be taken, always record this. The name of the person, department or company which undertook the action should be recorded. If possible an agreed date for the completion of the action should be given. The names of those who attended the meeting should be listed.

CHAIRING MEETINGS

One of the jobs most managers undertake from time to time is the chairing of meetings. It involves a public performance of doing your job. The fact you chair your meetings well may not improve your promotion prospects. If you make a mess of chairing meetings, word will get around and damage your prospects.

The first task of the chairman is to appoint someone to act as secretary to the meeting and to discuss the preliminaries with him. On the lower slopes of the pyramid you may not be in a position to appoint a secretary for the meeting. You may have to arrange the whole thing yourself. In this case you need to do all those things listed under the secretary's duties. It is extremely difficult to chair a meeting of any size and also take the minutes. You have to keep your attention on the meeting to control it. At the end of the meeting your notes may well be very sketchy.

To avoid problems it is worth asking someone else at the meeting to take the minutes or at least to take some notes for you. Failing this, you should recap at the end of the meeting and list all the agreed actions and decisions. It may well be worth doing this at the end of a meeting even if there is a secretary to take the minutes.

Throughout the meeting, the chairman must keep firmly in

There is nothing worse than a chairman who tries to run a meeting like a sergeant-major drilling a squad of new recruits

mind the purpose of the meeting. His aim must be to see that that purpose is fulfilled. He must control the meeting, keeping people to the point, keeping the discussion on a rational basis and calling a halt to any private conversations, which develop around the table. All this must be done as quietly and unobtrusively as possible. There is nothing worse than a chairman who is continually fussily interrupting or one who tries to run a business meeting like a sergeant major drilling a squad of new recruits.

As each agenda item is dealt with the chairman should make sure that it is clear what decision has been reached. He should also make sure that the actions which were agreed in the discussion, are clearly identified together with the name of the person who will take action and, if possible, a completion date. In some circumstances it may be useful for the chairman to make these points in a very brief summing up after each agenda item. This will certainly help the secretary. If the discussion has been at all confused it will also have the merit of clarifying the position for all present.

184

20

People

It is noticeable that top people seem to have a wide circle of
acquaintances. At the other extreme, a middle aged clerk or
labourer may have a very limited circle of acquaintances. You
can take a cynical view of this. Perhaps success and influence
attracts 'friends'. Perhaps failure or nonentity repel.

While there is certainly some truth in the cynical view, it is
perhaps too simple a view. It is like the chicken and the egg.
Which came first, success or the wide circle of acquaintances?
Some people start with some advantages. They may have
acquired a large number of acquaintances from their home,
school and university. Others may start their working life in a
strange town, knowing no one but their landlady and the person
they report to in their job. Both of these may be virtually total
strangers.

As we go through life, it is largely a matter of personal choice
whether we make friends and acquaintances. The choice may
be made unconsciously, but the choice is nonetheless there.
One essential for establishing personal relationships is time.
Busy men on their way to the top find this time. Many people
who stay near the bottom of the pyramid can never find time
for cementing personal relationships. There must be a lesson
to be learnt here.

NOT WHAT YOU KNOW BUT WHO YOU KNOW

How is it that busy people find the time? They are able to find the time because they organise their time properly and they allot a high priority to their dealings with people. They do this because they realise that people matter. They realise that they matter not only from humanitarian or religious reasons but in hard material terms. It is through people that you will achieve promotion. The organisational pyramid is similar in shape to those built by the Egyptians. It may even appear as stable, but throughout the pyramid there is a see-thing mass of humanity jockeying for position. The jockeying may become more polite as you reach the higher levels; it also becomes more ruthless and vicious. People owe their position in the pyramid to many things. One of the most important is the relationship they have built up with those around them — their equals, those above and below them in the pyramid.

It used to be said that in the race for promotion 'what matters is not what you know but who you know'. This originally referred to the practice of promoting friends and relatives rather than promoting on merit or qualifications. There is still some truth in the saying, but perhaps the emphasis is rather different. Even with the most highly organised system for selecting people for promotion, someone still has to make the recommendations. Someone has to make the final selection.

It is noticeable that some people get on easily with others. They find it natural to establish easy working relationships. They are the people who achieve results. Others have an un-happy knack of upsetting people. They create opposition where it does not already exist. Their achievements are slight. Most of us lie naturally between two extremes. As part of our plan for promotion we need to move ourselves over into the more effective group.

I mentioned above 'friends and business acquaintances'. I define a friend as someone whose interests I am prepared to put above my own and who in turn is prepared to put my interests above his own. There are not many friends in business — or anywhere else for that matter. Do not be de-ceived by the fact that some people appear to be very close — in and out of each others houses and spend a lot of time together. They may still just be acquaintances. They will help each other, keep each other informed and may form a very effective alliance until their personal interests conflict.

I emphasise this point because particularly near the bottom of the pyramid, you may feel you have several good friends. However, when it comes to competing for promotion, they will not concede any ground for you. They will use every opportunity to see that the promotion goes to them rather than to you or anyone else. This is not really very surprising, but be prepared.

As you know, you get 'nowt for nowt in this world and bloody little for sixpence'. This applies to personal relationships as much as anything else. The business world is not full of people of goodwill just waiting to help you in every possible way irrespective of what you do. You yourself have to make a positive effort to develop your relationships. I do not mean that you can buy acquaintances. The man who tries to buy friendship with his wallet is a pathetic sight. His acquaintances tend to disappear at the same time as his wallet. Establishing an effective circle of business acquaintances is a rather more subtle business. It involves basically a trading of support and information, though this is never spelt out.

REMEMBER NAMES AND FACES

To maintain reasonable relationships with people you meet, remember that they expect that you will take some interest in them, in what they do and what they say. The most basic way of showing no interest in someone is by failing to remember them or their name. To remember someone's appearance, the first essential is actually to take a good look at them, particularly their face. As I mentioned in Chapter 18 there are memory systems to help you with this.

Names often give difficulty. They are difficult to remember and to link with a face. This is particularly so where you only see someone very infrequently. One difficulty is that introductions are perfunctory. If on initially meeting someone you do not catch his name, say so and get him to repeat it. You can do this without offence when you first meet. I always write

peoples names down when I meet them. I find this helps me
to retain the name. If I meet a lot of strangers at a meeting, I
always draw a diagram of the seating and attach the names
to the seats. If I then refer to anyone who is present, I try
to refer to them by name. This both pleases them (provided
I get it right!) and helps to fasten name and face in my mind.

One particular point I find difficult is the person who has
a common christian name for a surname. I joined the Army
with a fellow recruit whose surname was Charlie. This gave
rise to some interesting exchanges between him and the NCO's.
If you occasionally meet a colleague called Sam Terry, it is
awkward when you accost him as Terry. It sounds very
patronising and no doubt irritates him. Both politeness and
self-interest suggest that you should make an effort to get
people's names right.

If you don't remember names, you can often bluff your way
through. If you have to take a newcomer into a gathering, you
cannot avoid the problem of introducing him. If the group
includes colleagues, who you do not see often and whose names
you cannot remember, you can be embarrassed and cause
offence. On the whole people feel better disposed to people
who address them by name rather than those who greet them
with an anonymous 'Good morning' or worse, 'Hello, old chap'.

As well as remembering names and faces, try to remember
something about the people you meet. At the very least
remember their job and where they work. Try to remember
what they tell you. If a man spends twenty minutes telling you
how well his daughter is doing at Oxford, he is likely to welcome an enquiry about her, next time you meet. He will feel
less friendly if you ask him how his daughter is doing with her
'O' levels. People in business, as elsewhere, like others to be
interested in them. Signs that you have been interested enough
to remember are appreciated.

Of course, if you are to remember what people say, you
have to give them an opportunity to say it in the first place.
A conversation is a two-way affair. You must give the other
person his turn to do the talking. If he is shy or just silent,
you can always encourage him to talk about himself. Certainly
you can avoid talking so hard that he has no opportunity to
talk. There are some people who prefer to keep their private

life totally separate from their business one. Avoid pushing them with questions about their private life and interests. You will only create offence. In practice most people, given the opportunity, need very little encouragement to talk about themselves.

YOUR INFORMAL NETWORK

If you work for a large organisation, you will find that you can work more effectively if you have an informal network of contacts throughout the organisation. You may only speak to someone two or three times in the year, but he may still be a useful source of support and of information. To some extent, useful contacts may be established haphazardly. The man who deliberately sets out to create and maintain such a network can make a more effective job of it.

It is easy enough to establish contact with people at your own place of work. Being pleasant, taking part in discussions, social and sporting events, remembering people's faces, names and jobs is sufficient to establish a wide circle of acquaintances here. Go out of your way to be helpful, take a positive attitude to other people's suggestions and avoid being obstructive. Remember that if you can look happy even when you aren't, you'll get on. Certainly the person who looks happy generally establishes more personal contacts more quickly than someone who looks perpetually dismal.

It is rather more difficult to make wider contacts. Certainly take every opportunity that is offered you to visit other parts of your company. Meetings in distant factories, involving an early start and late arrival home are unpopular and your seniors may well be glad to pass that opportunity on. Take it. It enables you to make contacts at the factory and may well enable you to make them at a more senior level than would otherwise be the case. If on trips of this kind you undertake to provide information or to do anything else, make sure you do it. It makes a good start to a relationship.

When visitors come to your office from distant parts of the company, try and be helpful. If they want to use a telephone, borrow a desk and chair, get some stationery or whatever, it is easy to provide it cheerfully or take them to someone who can provide it. You can of course decline because it is not your business to do it. But this is not very helpful and certainly will not help you plan for promotion.

Once on the lower rungs of management, the opportunities to improve your informal network improve. When the chance offers, you can accept people on transfer from other departments, and establishments of the company. Such people will still have friends in their old departments and links can be used to obtain information. Information obtained from good contacts on an informal basis is frequently more accurate and more timely than the information that becomes available down 'official channels'. Similarly if one of your staff wants a job elsewhere in the company, you could block the transfer because you can't spare him. It is normally much wiser to try to help him arrange the transfer and make the move at a time that is convenient to you. In doing this you will have helped both the man and his new boss. This extends your network.

Some managers are afraid of the people who work for them. They see them as potential rivals. They try to block their promotion and keep them where they are. This is a silly attitude and the man who adopts it has usually got as far as he is going to. You will be wiser. Encourage and train your people. If they are worth promotion, try and see they get it even if it means they are promoted to the same level as yourself. If they are promoted into jobs in other departments, you have once again extended your network.

As you go up the pyramid, you will find that people from your informal network, will call in to see you, when they visit the office, at which you work. If they give you no warning, this can be inconvenient. You may have urgent work to complete. You may be fully committed. You must, somehow, find the time to greet them in a friendly way and make them feel welcome. Try to spare a few minutes to chat to them and provide them with a cup of tea or coffee. Being unable to spare time for your acquaintances is the quickest way to lose them.

DEVELOP USEFUL OUTSIDE CONTACTS

Too many people live in a closed community within one company. This is a mistake and leads to a narrow outlook. In any case you may not wish to stay with one company for ever. Even if you want to, you may not have the opportunity to do so. Circumstances or the search for promotion may force a move. When you do want to move, it is a help to have contacts outside your own company.

It is not so much that these contacts will offer you jobs, though they may. It is more that they are a source of information and help. You will learn about opportunities and rewards elsewhere from them. They may provide you with useful introductions or references when you need them.

You may get the opportunity to go to meetings of trade associations, or chambers of commerce. You can join local clubs or organisations. You can attend the meetings of the local branch of the British Institute of Management and your professional body if you belong to one. By participating in the activities of these organisations you can extend your contacts well outside your own company.

Some people believe they should not be on friendly terms with people who work for rival firms. This is a fallacy. You will find people at the top of rival companies talking to each other in a friendly way on social occasions and co-operating together in common causes. There may be some carefully nurtured enmities but they tend to be the exception. Don't feel inhibited from making friends in rival companies. You will of course be careful not to give them confidential information about your company, but they will understand that this must be so.

There is no need to be obvious about declining to give confidential information. You can always plead ignorance or give an answer that avoids the question. It is fatuous to reply to a question 'Sorry. That's security information. I can't tell you.' It is an answer that creates tension and irritation unnecessarily. Just tactfully avoid the question and don't be afraid to say you don't know.

PERSONAL PR

One way of developing contacts outside your firm is to write or lecture about your work. If you are an expert in some sphere, you can write articles on that subject and offer them to the trade press. You will of course be wise to mention the matter to your boss before you send an article off. He may well want to read it before it goes. He may offer helpful criticism but at the least if he agrees to its going out, there should be no adverse comment in the company. He will also know whether your company operates any internal form of censorship, requiring that books and articles should be read and cleared by one of its PR staff. If you can establish yourself by writing articles as an expert on the work done by your department, this will certainly bring you some contacts and goodwill outside your own company. You may be asked to lecture by training establishments, or by other outside bodies.

There are a number of publishers specialising in publishing technical and management books. If you can write several articles, the chances are that you could write a book. I had written very little for publication when I decided with my friend and colleague John Taylor, to write a book on project management. We were both project managers at the time and came to the conclusion that no book was available that covered the market.

We discussed the possibility with the Editorial Director of Business Books, who expressed interest and asked us to provide him with a synopsis and two specimen chapters. After looking at these, he gave us a contract to write the book. After *Successful Project Management* was published we made a number of interesting outside contacts. The editor of *Accountancy,* the journal of the Institute of Chartered Accountants asked us to write an article for them. The Institution of Electrical Engineers asked us to lecture at their summer school. We were also asked to lecture to a number of other organisations. Finally Business Books asked us to write another book on project management, *Practical Project Management.* I tell you this to illustrate the sort of contacts that arise out of writing a book. As a result of writing *Successful Project Management,* John Taylor and I met or corresponded with about two hundred or so people outside our own organisation. By the time we had written it, we knew a lot more about project management, our job, than when we started.

The outside contacts may not have been of great direct use, but they have certainly been of considerable interest. Do not expect that you will make much money from either writing or lecturing on technical subjects. You will learn from doing so and if you're lucky you will meet some interesting people as a result.

People are important in your plan for promotion. Whether your route upwards lies through management or through some specialist line, your success will be greatly affected by the way you get on with people, by the extent of your informal network of contacts and by its effectiveness.

21

Your People

People are at the root of every success and failure. Your
future promotion depends on people of all sorts. Perhaps
the most important people of all are those who work for
you — or who will work for you in the future.

You may not yet have anyone working for you. This is an
ideal starting point from which to study the subject. Observe
how your boss treats you and how you react to him. Watch
other managers; see how they treat their staff and what
response they get. Study the official notices and announce-
ments and note your own reactions and those of other
people.

Even if you do have people working for you, you can still
study your own reactions to your boss. How does he criticise,
praise and help you? How do you react? Above all look out
for the smooth running efficient department, which always
meets its targets. How is it managed?

KEY TO YOUR SUCCESS

There may be great men who succeed entirely by their own
efforts. They tend to follow artistic occupations. Certainly
in large organisations, no man succeeds solely by his own
efforts. He succeeds as a result of his own efforts plus the

support and effort of the people who work for him. No man works his way up an organisation on his own.

Broadly speaking, people work their way up the pyramid because they produce results. There are a lot of other factors but the foundation for successful progress up that pyramid is results. The results expected vary from organisation to organisation, but whatever those results are, the key to promotion lies in delivering them.

At the bottom of the pyramid you may produce results by concentration and hard work. By the time you are responsible for the work of several other people, you will not be able to produce good results without their help and co-operation. This is the most important aspect of management and one for which some companies provide no preparation at all.

As you start up the management or supervisory ladder you need to study how to manage your people and how to get results from them. Particularly on the lower rungs, they can by one means or another bring about a rapid change in your promotion prospects.

There are many different styles of management. Some managers behave like nursemaids. They issue detailed instructions about everything and are constantly checking on their subordinates. They have a careful system for the checking of all work so that as few mistakes as possible will show outside the department. Some are martinets. They expect punctuality, keep meal and rest breaks strictly and issue instructions in clear staccato style. Some managers are slave drivers. They work their people as hard as they know how. They squeeze their people for more output. They get as much unpaid overtime out of their people as possible. Some managers apply the mushroom management principle: 'Keep 'em in the dark and pour plenty of muck over them'. Yet other managers are over-anxious to please their staff. They give the minimum of instructions. They turn a blind eye to poor time-keeping. They allow padding of expense claims and sometimes authorise payment for overtime that has not been worked. Some managers are consistent about what they expect from their staff. Others are not. Managers come in all shapes and sizes and so do their management styles.

I believe you will get the best results from your people if

195

you give them their heads, within limits. If possible define their work and set them objectives with targets to be hit by certain dates. Don't let those dates be too far ahead. Make sure you have explained to each man or woman who works for you what you expect from them. Tell them their purpose in the organisation. Encourage them to think on the job and to do their work without constantly running to you for rulings or guidance. Give them the opportunity to perform.

If you want to get the best from your people, you should study the subject. A very good starting point is John Humble's book *'Improving Business Results'*. This gives a basic description of management by objectives and is available in paperback (published by Pan).

For many people on their way up, particularly specialist staff, the first person they have to work for them is a secretary. Others may acquire a large staff before they get their own secretary. Regrettably over the years secretaries have come to be seen as a status symbol. Some managers therefore insist on having a secretary even if they do not need one. When you get a secretary make a resolution to use her properly.

A secretary is not just a shorthand typist. She should be an extension of yourself and used to the greatest extent possible to relieve you of routine duties, hence helping you to accumulate those chunks of time you need to do effective work. Get her to write your routine letters. There is no point in dictating letters to her, if she can compose them herself. You simply go through the mail and write a brief instruction on each letter and memo and give it back to her. With a more experienced secretary the process can be reversed. She deals with all the routine and merely asks you for guidance on those where she needs your guidance or thinks you may wish to exercise a personal choice.

Girls who are qualified to take shorthand normally like to get a fair amount of dictation. Unfortunately, however, it is a pretty uneconomic way of getting letters and reports written. Few people dictate anything more than simple letters well. These the secretary ought to be able to write for herself. With longer or more complicated matters it is difficult to dictate something that will read well. You can of course dictate a draft, correct it by hand and have it re-typed. However, you

*Managers come in all shapes and sizes and so
do their management styles*

might as well do that into a dictating machine and leave your
secretary free to get on with her other work. Indeed, a dictating machine may well be a piece of equipment which allows
you to considerably increase your effectiveness.

With a good secretary you need to build up some form of
personal relationship. By that I do not mean that you should
start a flirtation or sexual relationship with her. You should
however try to strike a reasonably friendly note. Give her a
present at Christmas. Listen to her gossip. If she normally
works to suit you and stays on when you need her to, then
reciprocate. Let her off early when she is going to a party.
Allow her out to have her hair done during the day. In short,
be human and friendly with her.

SELECT THEM CAREFULLY

When you are promoted or transferred you normally have no option but to accept the people who worked for your predecessor. In some organisations, managers have very little say over who works for them. There are centrally controlled recruiting policies and programmes. Internal transfers and promotions follow a complicated ritual, which may mean that a manager has to do the best he can with what he is given.

In most of private industry the individual manager has more scope. He is of course still faced with accepting the staff in position when he first takes up his appointment. He may also be over-ruled by his manager in matters of transfers and promotions. Normally however he has more scope.

When you are allowed to expand your existing staff or when you set up a completely new department, you have an opportunity, which you should take. You have an opportunity to select people to fill your needs. If you bring the right people in and look after them, you will have a special relationship which should be beneficial to you. So don't muff it by letting other people do the selecting for you.

Particularly if you are setting up a new department, you may be very busy and tempted to let the personnel department do the selection for you. Resist the temptation. This is one occasion upon which overtime is fully justified. You should interview and select every one who will report directly to you. You should also interview and give the final OK on everyone at the next level down.

If you have no experience of interviewing then you should certainly try to get some as early as you can. The art of interviewing is so important that some companies run their own short courses on the subject. Some companies also have open evenings, when they invite people to come in for informal interviews in order to decide whether or not there might be opportunities for them in the company. These informal interviews often coincide with a trade fair or exhibition.

Personnel managers sometimes have difficulty in finding interviewers for these informal interview sessions. It often involves working late into the evening. These sessions provide a good opportunity to get some experience of real life interviewing. For actual job interviews there a number of techniques can be used. One technique, a seven-point plan is given in some detail in *The Basic Arts of Management* by John Taylor and myself (published by Business Books).

Be very careful about internal transfers from other parts of the company. The transferee may have a good reason for wanting a transfer. His manager may have a good reason for letting him go. It is just possible that you are being passed a dud or a misfit. If you collect too many duds, you will find it hard to run an effective department. If your department does not run effectively and produce results, you may as well say goodbye to that promotion plan.

The fact that a man performs badly under one manager does not mean that he is inevitably a bad acquisition for you. His bad performance may have been due to poor management, the type of work he was employed on or a clash of personalities.

Nonetheless, it pays to be careful. This is a situation in which your informal network can prove useful. You may be able to get useful comments on the man and his managers. You should at least get an idea as to whether the reasons given for wanting a transfer are genuine or not.

COACH THEM

There are several reasons why you should train and coach your staff. We saw, earlier in this book, that the only person responsible for your development, was yourself. Notwithstanding that conclusion, you should still accept responsibility for developing your staff. Even if you look at it from a purely selfish viewpoint, it is worth doing so.

The first point is that you should never allow yourself to become indispensible in your job. If you do you may be passed over for promotion because you cannot be spared. The second is that your seniors when assessing you for promotion will be looking, among other things, at your ability to manage and develop people. Thirdly, your people will work more effectively if they are properly trained and developed rather than if they are not. They are also likely to respond to

199

the personal interest you show in them. Fourthly, the more they are developed, the more of your work they can do. This helps to cut out overtime for you and also leaves you with time to accept jobs delegated by your boss and to spend on special projects.

Particularly in the initial stages, the development of your staff will take up a significant amount of your time. Some improvement of your peoples' performance may be obtained by sending them on training courses. Some improvement can be obtained by encouraging them to read of modern methods in the trade press and in technical books. However, the major contribution to their development should lie in personal coaching on the job. You should do the coaching.

Just as your boss is the most important influence on your career, so you are the most important influence on the future careers of your subordinates. On training courses, many students complain that although they have found the course interesting, it has no real relevance to their job. If you actually coach them on the job, this must have immediate and direct relevance. This fact is also clearly seen by the person being trained. There is a lot more to coaching than arranging for the person concerned to 'sit by Nelly and see what she does'.

The possibility of coaching your people should always be in your mind. You may, however, be a fair way up the pyramid before it is possible. To coach effectively you should work to a plan rather than haphazardly. The most effective method of coaching is delegation. This should not be done in a random uncontrolled way. Nor should you just throw your subordinates into the deep end and watch to see if they sink or swim.

Start delegation carefully, one thing at a time. Even the extent of the delegation on this one thing may be limited at first so that any decision is discussed with you before it is finally made. However the aim must be to delegate completely. This means delegation of decisions as well as routine work. It will mean accepting those decisions as your own. It also means that some mistakes will also be made and you must accept responsibility for those too.

When you delegate an area of work or some particular problem or project, do not leave it at that. Review progress

200

with the man from time to time. This should not be a session in which you sit and criticise what he has done. Your aim should be to persuade him to think about the job, not just to do it. Get him to explain how he tackled a particular problem and why he did it in that particular fashion. Discuss alternative ways of tackling the problem with him. Try to get him to do the thinking and ask the questions.

As part of your development programme for your people, you can — to use an American expression — rotate them, i.e. within your own section or department, switch them between jobs. This broadens their experience and gives them a better view of the work of the department as a whole. It also has the incidental benefit that the department can cope effectively when you lose people through sickness, holiday or transfer.

Part of coaching is to broaden the outlook of your people. An effective way of doing this is to start taking them into your confidence on your decisions, how and why you are making them. You can sometimes take them to meetings with you, so that they meet a wider circle of people outside your own department and so that they get a better grasp of the range of factors influencing your work.

I have always found that teaching other people is one of the best ways of learning. So, in coaching your staff, you are not only developing them but developing yourself as well. Another method of development I like is to set aside a short period each month for training, for the key half dozen people working for you. You can get each one of them to read a book a month. They can then make a short presentation of the ideas they have gleaned from the book to their colleagues at the monthly training session. General discussion of each presentation can be directed to the question of whether or not the ideas can be applied in your own department.

LOOK AFTER THEM

Developing and coaching your people is just one aspect of looking after your people. When the people that work for you have a problem that affects them at work, hopefully you should be the first person they turn to. You have a responsibility for looking after them. Large organisations can be very inhuman. They can make rules that sometimes bear very hardly on some individuals. In such circumstances you must be prepared to look after the interests of your people and not just abandon them to the machine.

The working conditions and pay of the people who work for you must be a matter for your concern. You may work for a very formally structured company which allows very little scope to the individual manager particularly at the junior level. But in many companies, you will have scope. The people that work for you will appreciate — and work better for — even quite minor interventions on your part. Perhaps the central heating is normally turned on on 1 October. On 25 September it is freezing in the office. The poor manager accepts it, the good one does something about it — pesters the office administrator or senior management till he gets the heat switched on (particularly if the temperature is below the legal minimum).

Perhaps the procedure for reclaiming expenses is time-consuming and people are kept waiting for their money; maybe the office lighting is poor; perhaps the tea-ladies bring round cool tea; perhaps the lavatories are dirty. Minor things of this sort may not be your direct responsibility. However if they affect the people who work for you, then they should be of concern to you. Your people will expect you to be 'fair'; fair in dealing with their claims on you and on the company; and fair between them — there should be no favouritism. Benefits or privileges given to one person should be seen to have been earned.

You should never expect any of your people to accept responsibility for your mistakes or for your faulty decisions. There is nothing which brings a manager into disrepute with his people more quickly than trying to shuffle responsibility for his own mistakes onto his staff.

There may be times when your people have off periods. They may be distracted or concerned by some private worry. It is no business of yours to pry into their private lives. However, if a normally effective worker goes temporarily off the rails, look below the surface for the cause. Don't be censorious. Try instead to explore the trouble with the person to help them see how they can get their performance back to normal.

Some managers somehow always manage to do a little bit better for their people. Whenever there are additional benfits going, they get them. When wages and salaries go up, their people always seem to get the best deal. Such managers rarely have difficulty in getting and retaining staff. This is so even if they expect their people to work harder than most. It is so even if they are strict about time-keeping and intolerant of slackness. People work for such managers because they know they are good managers to work for. They look after their people. You should do the same.

From time immemorial leaders have risen on the backs of their supporters. These leaders have earned privilege, power and wealth. The wise ones have remembered their supporters. A reputation for looking after his supporters never harmed any leader — or any manager.

After your own drive and determination, the people who work for you can be the most effective force to help you up the pyramid. You will expect loyalty from them. Do not forget that you owe them a loyalty too.

22

Your Home Base

Throughout this book I have concentrated on the working environment in which you will make and follow your plan for promotion. A very important factor is bound to be your home life. Your home is the castle from which you go out to conquer the world. It is the refuge you come back to, to lick your wounds and to rest and recuperate.

In some respects you start your working life with an existing home background and commitments. As the years go on and — hopefully — you rise up the pyramid you are able to make some choices. You can choose in which of several directions you intend to go.

BUILD YOUR OWN INDEPENDENCE

As you work your way up your own particular pyramid you do not want to be completely dependent on the company that employs you. If for any reason you want to leave the company or it wants to fire you, you should be able to face the prospect with equanimity. You will only be able to do so if you have built up a degree of independence.

Although financial independence is important, it is not the only form of independence you need. You need to keep yourself in such a position that you could always get another job, if you had to; indeed not just another job but another job at least as good or better than the one you've got. One young man I knew when I started my life in business stayed with the same company for many years. Every two years or so, he would study the job advertisements, select one or more jobs that he liked the look of. He would apply for these and carry the application through to the point at which he got an offer or refusal. At that stage he would judge the offered job against his probable prospect in his current job. If they seemed better, he would take the letter of offer along to his boss and ask his advice on the matter.

Not everyone has the same brass neck as he had, but it may still be quite a good idea just to try the job market from time to time. It indicates whether or not you are currently paid the market rate, for what you have to offer. It also keeps your hand in. There is of course the problem of turning down the offers in a tactful way that does not close that particular company's doors to you for ever.

The fact that you have succeeded in obtaining a good offer of alternative employment within the last two years can be a help to you in facing out awkward situations in your own company.

To retain your own marketability you must avoid letting your skills and knowledge become obsolescent or too one-company oriented. Whatever your special skills, in accountancy, engineering, administration, management or whatever, it is important to keep up to date. This is easily done if you have a wide circle of acquaintances outside the company with whom you can discuss business matters. It is also important to keep up any membership of a professional institution. As you progress into line management, you should qualify for membership of the British Institute of Management and join it. Keep up with your reading both of professional and management journals and of new books.

The other foundation for independence — finance — also needs consideration. At the start of one's career there is always plenty of temptation to live beyond one's means. It would be nice to have a bigger house, a better car, smarter holidays, more clothes or whatever. There is always a temptation to spend the next rise before we get it, as well as forgetting that it will be subject to tax.

I believe that if you are going to establish a firm home base, you need to live within your income and to devote some part of your income to saving. You need to build up a reserve fund, which will support you for a reasonable period if you do suddenly part company with your present employers. If you have a reserve fund, this gives you time to look for the right job and not just take the first you can get because you need the money.

The size of such a reserve needs to be related to your age and family commitments. It is probably easiest to think of it in terms of so many months spending. In your 20s, it is probably sufficient to have an emergency reserve to cover three months' normal spending. By the time you are 50, changing jobs is more difficult, your emergency reserve should probably be enough for a year's spending.

Quite apart from your emergency reserve fund, it is sensible to have a contingency plan and keep it up to date. What do you need to do if . . .? Which of your contacts will be useful in finding another job? Who should you tell if you leave your job? Who needs to be given your home 'phone number and address so that they can contact you? If you have a company car, occupy a company flat or have your children's schooling paid for by the company, what are your plans for dealing with the situation if you left the company? All these points and many more particular to your own case should be thought about and reviewed at least once a year.

YOUR FINANCES

Your finances extend to more than the establishment of an emergency reserve. The first aspect of your finances you should thoroughly understand is the full range of financial benefits available to you from your company. You may think this is obvious but do you know what your widow would get from your company if you died tonight?

Some people have so much paper to deal with at work that they cannot stomach the thought of keeping personal files. You should at least keep some files. The first should contain every letter or notice from your employer in which he has set out your pay and conditions of service or variations to them. If you work for the sort of organisation where you can get a copy of your annual assessment or report, you should file a copy of this too. You should also keep a file of everything to do with your pension scheme and all letters and instructions dealing with benefits your firm provides. It is also quite a good idea to keep an old shoe box to house all your payslips. To make it easy to find them, I put each years slips in a separate envelope in the box.

Apart from retaining the papers, you should also understand them. A surprisingly large number of people do not really understand how their net pay is made up. They know the general principles but do not know the details and rarely if ever bother to check up. You should start by understanding how your gross pay is calculated. It may be a single straightforward monthly sum. But many people are paid a basic salary with fairly complicated additions for performance or overtime. It is important to understand how these additions are calculated. Salary offices can make mistakes. Also someone, like a sales manager, who receives occasional quite large bonuses, may be able to reduce his tax bill if he understands how to smooth his income over successive tax years. It is in any case advisable to understand how your tax and other deductions are calculated. Mistakes happen here as well. A sudden demand for £100 because a mistake has been repeated month by month for the last two years can be a nasty shock. *Money Which,* one of the Consumer Association's publications, devotes one issue a year to reviewing the tax situation. This is an excellent guide and will provide all the information you need to understand most income tax problems. The address of the Consumer Association Subscription Department is Caxton Hill, Hertford SG13 7LZ.

Perhaps the least understood part of your remuneration is your company-provided life assurance and pension. A lot of people don't like to ask too much about these matters. They are afraid they will seem too security conscious and earn a black mark. Pension and life assurance are just as much a part of the pay for your work as your salary is. Details vary wildly from company to company. You should get a copy of the rules, if they are not issued automatically, and read them. You will be wise to be quite clear about what options will be open to you if you leave the company before normal retirement age; what happens if you have to leave work due to sickness or death; how is your final pension calculated? If after you have read the rules, you don't understand your situation, then ask.

Nearly every manager is concerned with money as part of his job. He has to produce forecasts and estimates. He works to a budget and is given regular comparisons of actual expenditure against budget. He is continually concerned about profits, margins and costs. Yet, perhaps as a reaction of relief, very many managers hardly give any organised thought to their personal finances. Money flows in regularly and is promptly spent. You owe it to yourself to give at least as much attention to your own finances as you do to your company's.

As a minimum you should produce an annual budget, a comparison of actual expenditure against budget and an annual statement of net assets. Backing this you should have a financial plan, which links with your plan for promotion. This should set out your financial objectives and how you plan to achieve them. Life in business management is a chancy business. Companies go bust, firms are taken over, technologies change and managerial palace revolutions take place. These can inject an element of uncertainty into the best of promotion plans. Your financial plan should aim to counteract some of the uncertainty.

A civil servant or other public servant with virtually complete security of tenure, fixed salary scales and a salary that is almost guaranteed inflation-proof in normal circumstances, can plan his finances quite precisely over many years ahead. He can spend every last penny of his income, knowing that his salary will arrive without fail next month and the month after right to the end of his service. When that end comes in the fullness of time, he will receive a pension related to his final salary and that pension itself will be largely inflation-proof. He will also get a capital payment to float him off on his retirement.

The business manager must face much more uncertainty. You will be wise to follow Mr Micawber's advice and live comfortably within your income. In that way you will save yourself a lot of worry and enhance your happiness. It will also enable you to gradually build up some capital. You will be wise to examine rationally all the risks you face and consider to what extent you should try to cover them by insurance. Certainly anyone with a wife and young family should make sure they will be adequately provided for in the event of death or disablement.

In time of inflation, I believe the first use of capital should be to buy your own house. Even at the time of writing, when property values are falling, your own house is still about the best investment there is and is certainly a better store of value than any form of money. Within limits, it probably pays to get the largest mortgage you can and to buy the best house you can. I believe that having done that you should pay off the mortgage as rapidly as possible. Once you own the roof over your head, free of mortgage, you have achieved a major element of independence.

My view is contrary to the accepted view which says secure your mortgage against an endowment policy and if possible run the mortgage at its full size until you retire. Inflation will see that it becomes a decreasing burden. This was true enough in the first 30 years after World War Two, but may not currently be as valid. The man, who is free of debt, must have more independence of action and less to fear from the cessation of his job. Contrary to some beliefs, the higher you rise in business and politics, the more insecure your tenure.

Some managers would argue that my whole emphasis on house ownership is wrong. They — and they are mostly Americans — would argue that ownership of a house makes you too immobile, too inclined to put down roots. I am sure that their attitude is wrong in the conditions that apply in Britain. Owning a sound modern house is one of the few genuine ways of protecting your capital against erosion by inflation. Rented accommodation is very hard to find in modern Britain and, if anything, the flat renter is less mobile than the house owner.

After securing a house and furnishing it, I believe your first claim on your savings should be the establishment of the emergency fund I referred to earlier. This should be invested in such a way that you can always obtain the money at face value quickly. A building society share account with one of the big societies like the Abbey National or Nationwide is as good a place as any. You might get a higher rate of interest elsewhere but these societies have the advantage of security and prompt repayment if you need it at short notice.

Only after you have equipped yourself with adequate life insurance, a house and an emergency fund should you be tempted into more adventurous and potentially more profitable investments. If you do reach the stage where you have money to spare for investment — and risk — in unit trusts, the stock markets or commodity futures markets, make sure you understand what is involved before you start. You might find *Personal Finance for Managers* a useful starting point. John Taylor and I wrote it and it was published by Business Books.

YOUR HEALTH

Your most important asset is not a financial one. It is your health. Many managers sacrifice it in the struggle for promotion. You can do nothing to guarantee that you will retain good health. There are some things you can do to avoid preventable ill health.

The first essential is to continue to get adequate exercise after you start out in business. It is very easy, particularly if you are studying for a professional qualification as well as doing a full days work, to get out of the way of taking any exercise. Later when you are well established in your job, it is equally easy to go from your home front door to your office door by car. You can find yourself in a situation where the only exercise on weekdays is walking from your office to the dining room. Some regular exercise is essential to good health.

You should try to walk two to three miles every day. Use the office stairs instead of the lift. Try to keep up at least one sport. It is a good idea to take up some sport early in life, which you can keep up almost into old age. Golf is one popular sport, which provides plenty of fresh air and exercise and can be played well in to your sixties or beyond. My own preference is for dinghy sailing. There are few places in Britain or Western Europe that are far from sailable water. Dinghy sailing also has the great merit that once out in a boat it is easy to forget your landborn worries. A successful day competing with other sailors or just with the elements can be a great restorer of the spirits. It costs some money but is not as expensive as many people think.

Combined with exercise is the need to keep your weight down to its proper level. Excess weight slows you down mentally and physically. It also seems to be associated with a high incidence of certain diseases such as coronary thrombosis. The answer to the problem of keeping your weight down is simple. Take plenty of exercise and don't eat too much. Find out the right weight for someone of your height and build. Life insurance companies issue tables giving this information. Failing that your doctor can give you a figure. Try to keep to it. If you are involved in much business entertaining you can build up weight very quickly. As a junior sales manager, I used to eat lunch three or four times a week with customers or prospective customers. When I got home my wife would have a full evening meal ready for me. Within a few months I became quite fat.

This was not really necessary. I started to cut out the roll and butter and all potatoes from the business lunch. I also cut out the biscuits I ate every time I had tea or coffee during the day. Keeping your weight down is largely a matter of self-discipline. If the company is paying for your lunch, it is not difficult to avoid starchy items and stick to the higher cost, high protein items. It is not a bad idea to equip yourself with a set of bathroom scales, so that you can keep an eye on the situation.

Allied with overeating as a source of managerial ill health is overdrinking. This is a particular hazard for those engaged in sales and public relations. Beer can do as much to add to your weight as potatoes. Even if you do not have to drink as part of your job, you may well feel entitled to a drink with your lunch and a couple when you get home to help you relax. Alcoholism is a serious disease. Alcohol is an addictive

Equip yourself with a set
of bathroom scales

drug. Moderate drinking will not produce serious results but a particular jolt or worry can start you on the path from moderate drinking to excess. If you do drink regularly, it is not a bad idea to give it a holiday from time to time if only to show yourself you still can.

Smoking is not only a long-term killer, it is also a producer of fug and office pollution. It is not necessary either to drink or smoke. Both are acquired tastes and many people acquire them because they think it is the right thing to do. They are both habits worth dropping in earlier life. If you do you will be both physically and financially healthier.

Senior managers can spend a lot of time travelling. There is always a temptation to get as near a full days work in as possible. Managers are tempted to start early and get home late. If they are away overnight, they tend to work, write notes or hold discussions on the nights they are away from home. This is tiring and eventually has an impact on their health. It can also affect their family.

FAMILY AND LIFESTYLE

If you have a wife and family — or intend to have one in the future — remember the impact your plan for promotion will have on them. What benefits will it bring them? What disadvantages will they suffer? Will your wife have to play an active part? Will she for instance, have to entertain or travel with you? Will your wife be forced into the position of complete responsibility for your children and home because you do not spare the time for your share? Will the requirements of your plan make it impossible or difficult for your wife to have a career of her own. If so, will she be happy about it?

You should ask yourself all these questions as you pursue your plan for promotion. From time to time you should sit back, review your plan and ask yourself whether the results are worth the costs. Just as you examine your priorities at work, so you should examine your priorities between home and work. Some managers sacrifice their family and their relationship with their family in order to keep moving up that pyramid.

Make sure that you do take your annual holidays in full. You need them to recover your energy and to enjoy your family. You may sometimes have to work late, bring work home or work at the weekends. This may be inevitable if you are aiming high. However do try to avoid making too much of a habit of it.

Your home and your family should be the secure base from which you go out to work. It should be there, secure as ever, not only to receive you at the end of your working day but also at the end of your working life. It is worth ensuring your home base is not destroyed by your single-minded concentration on your plan for promotion.

Part Four

SUMMING UP

23

Promotion — a Crucial Factor in Company Success

Like so much else, you do not find people to promote by chance. Promotion is a matter affecting every member of an organisation, whether directly or indirectly. Yet the individual's interest in promotion is not necessarily the same as the organisation's. To some extent their interests may be in conflict.

There are many claims on top management time. Yet both the mechanics and policy for promotion are too important to leave to the personnel department. Senior managers will of course be interested in the selection of their immediate subordinates and in grooming their successors but their interest should go much further than this.

Promotion policy itself is closely linked to the very framework of an organisation. Both policy and mechanics lie close to the heart of any organisation and have an important effect on motivation. The Chief Executive of any organisation needs to devote some of his time to meeting, encouraging and evaluating those managers at all levels, who are highly graded for promotion. The mere fact that he is aware of the excellent gradings and that he comments on them directly to the man or woman concerned can be an important additional motivating factor.

It is important to be clear on the objectives of promotion policy and practise. Primarily promotion policy is concerned with securing the succession and ensuring the continuity of the organisation. It should be concerned with the future rather than with the past. In other words when you select someone for promotion it is in the expectation that he or she will do the new job well and indeed that they are the best person available to do it. It is not a reward for past services.

This line may easily become blurred because the most important evidence about how a man or woman will perform in the future lies in their past achievement. The manager doing the selecting must be clear in his own mind about this. It may be very difficult in practice particularly for promotions near the top of the ladder. Yet it is even more important here as there is no room for passengers at this level if the organisation is to survive. If you have worked for many years with a man, who has consistantly been successful, it is very hard to pass him over and promote someone in his place when you judge he would reach his level of incompetance with the promotion. There is always a strong temptation to at least give him the chance.

Another important aspect of promotion policy is the need to make the best possible use of the human resources available to an organisation. This is not a mere humanitarian or philanthropic gesture. For once, profit, humanity and even philanthropy may desire the same objective — the full development of each person in the organisation and their most effective use in the organisation. It is fairly common in some organisations to complain that there is insufficient management potential in an organisation and as a consequence to recruit people from outside to fill a high proportion of senior posts. Too much external recruitment for senior jobs has a demotivating effect on existing staff.

Equally importantly, it is difficult to judge the potential recruit accurately and to make sure he is really right for the job. No one would select a first-rate pilot to manage an aircraft factory. There are more subtle difficulties. It is claimed that management skills are easily transferable between organisations and even between public and private sector or between large and small companies. Such moves in practice do not always go well. The large company senior manager may have used a more limited range of skills than are needed in the managing director of a small or medium firm. He may also have a different style of management inappropriate to the smaller organisation. When you want to attract someone from outside the organisation, there has to be something in it for the recruit. If this is merely more money there is probably little problem apart from distortions and anomalies in the pay structure. However, the recruit may only be attracted by the promise of a bigger job. The top designer of one company may be offered the job of development director of his new company. Once again we run into the Peter Principle. External recruiting can be risky. The more senior the job, the greater the risk.

I have written in Part Two about the importance of groups that form and move together. When a manager moves from one organisation into a senior job in another organisation he may be tempted to take 'his group' with him after a decent interval. This may ostensibly be necessary in order to over-come the shortcomings of existing staff; because his friends need the money; or most likely because he finds he needs them in order to manage in the style to which he has become accustomed. In the course of their transposition from one organisation to the other, some members of the group may be promoted into inappropriate jobs.

It is important to watch out for the formation of promo-tion chains. There may be no harm in them. On the other hand they may represent a group moving up the organisation together. So long as they work effectively together you may feel that no harm is done. However many groups contain some people who are not particularly effective. In the origins of the group they may have had some key skill or contact, but may no longer actually contribute anything to the group except loyalty. Promotion practice must aim to keep such people at their proper level of effectiveness.

Promotion policy is not just a matter of steering people in an uninterruptedly upward fashion. It must be concerned with sideways moves both to broaden people's experience and to move them to more appropriate jobs. Most difficult of all, it must also deal with demotions. Individuals sometimes make the mistake of allowing greed, ignorance or ambition to take them beyond their level of competence. To some extent senior management take a risk every time they promote someone. Indeed, they should do so. If promotions are always made on a safety-first policy the organisation is likely to stagnate. Some risks must be taken, however carefully managers are coached for more senior jobs. Mistakes will be made and people promoted into jobs they cannot do effectively. The mistake must be rectified by training by moving to an alternative post at the same level or by demotion.

There is nothing more destructive of an organisation than managers who are not up to their job. Apart from the direct results, they produce a chain of unhappy consequences. The key factor with demotion is that it should be done humanely. When a person is demoted, he should not be destroyed. His pride may be affronted, but he may recognise his own shortcomings and wish to move down if only it can be done without outward signs of disgrace. Moving down should be almost as easy as moving up. The existence of outward marks of status makes this more difficult. If demotion involves dining in the 4th tier lunch room instead of the 3rd tier lunch room; if it involves giving up a company car or reserved car park space if it involves moving from a private office into a large general office; then the effects of the demotion itself is compounded by a public slap on the face. It may be better both for the organisation and for the man himself if he leaves the organisation. However it is better if the demotion can be carried out discreetly and without fuss. The actual change of role and authority must of course be clear out but it need not be accompanied by public humiliation. This may seem trivial particularly when you observe it in other people. When you are yourself the subject of demotion, it gives the matter a different perspective. The less the outward trappings of promotion, the easier it will be to demote and still bring the demoted person back into effective production. When someone is demoted, he should not be shunted into a siding where it he has insufficient to do and consequently becomes a centre of disaffection. I believe that on demotion a man should be offered the option of voluntary redundancy and helped to find a job outside the organisation if he wants to go. If he opts to stay, his next job should be selected for him, as carefully as if he were being promoted. It should be a job he has already proved he can do. He should be moved into the job and given stretching objectives. This will keep him too busy to mope and, providing he is successful, will help to rebuild his self-confidence. To others in the company it may appear that the job he has moved into is an important one, for which he was the best suited candidate. This helps maintain both his self-respect and his credibility with his colleagues. If people have to be demoted because they cannot cope with a job and provided it is not directly their fault, there is a strong case for not cutting their salary on the demotion. He may well have moved his expenditure up into line with the higher salary and told his wife and family about it. Particularly for those with long service in the organisation, it may be better to allow time and inflation to erode the salary to that commensurate with the more junior job. If you can not believe it necessary to be humane in this, recognise that it may still be a wise — and very minor — investment in a contented well motivated work force.

Traditionally one of the reasons for over promotion, and hence the need for demotion, has been the steepness of the promotion pyramid and the narrowness of the route to the top. Specialists have been forced to choose between doing the job they enjoy and are good at and doing the management job, which will bring them money, promotion and status. Part of the care therefore lies in providing parallel promotion paths, which allow individuals to satisfy their ambitions in the way that is of greatest use to the organisation. We should set out to harness peoples ambitions not to stifle them. As Sir Henry Taylor wrote over a century ago, 'Hardly anything will bring a man's mind into full activity if ambition be wanting'.

An important aspect of any promotion policy is that it must be both fair and seen to be fair. It must offer the prospect of promotion to everyone in the organisation. No one with the potential for promotion should be overlooked.

There is one particular area where I believe many organisations overlook the possibility of finding good people for junior and middle management. This is particularly true of those organisations with well structured promotion structures.

A great deal of emphasis is placed on catching people young and developing them. In the process some people are overlooked. Their main interests may lie outside their job, perhaps in travel, sport or social matters. They may have changed their jobs several times to fit their outside interests. Some of these people find themselves in their 40s in lowly jobs, which do not stretch them at all. Some have considerable potential, but they have been written off — after all they can't really be suitable for promotion to a more responsible job. If they were, it would have happened years ago. Their aspirations have gradually been crushed out of them. As Sir Henry Taylor put it: 'The hope and not the fact of advancement is the spur to industry'. No one, who has several years to go before retirement, should see his promotion path totally blocked. It is demoralising. Apart from that, you may really be overlooking a considerable pool of talent. Any promotion policy should provide for those who wish (and are capable) to re-enter the race. Indeed, a good manager will encourage and coach his middle-aged potential. These people if adequately motivated can provide a degree of stability and staying power. Uncultivated they provide a layer of negative attitudes and may even become centres of serious disaffection. It takes time to re-inspire the 40 year old with the necessary confidence and to train him. In many ways this may still be more rewarding than training the graduate entry. The late developer is more likely to remain with you and to feel some obligation to the organisation.

Good managers and good leaders are sufficiently scarce to make it worth combing all levels of your organisation for them. Having found the potential it pays to develop it. If you complain now that you have no good people coming on in your organisation, it is probably your own fault. It results from policies followed — if only by default — over a period of years.

If you are short of good managers by all means recruit externally to fill the immediate vacancies. More importantly you should review your promotion policies and practices to ensure that in future you only have to hire from outside that proportion of managers necessary to prevent your organisation from becoming too introverted.

24

Your Success in the Promotion Stakes: the Golden Rules

In Part Two I suggested some of the aspects of promotion which should concern companies. In Part Three I suggested how you may plan your own promotion. In this chapter I outline a few golden rules to guide you along your promotion path.

1   *'Take care to get what you like or you will be forced to like what you get.'* So wrote George Bernard Shaw. You need to clear your own mind about what you want. This is the first essential step towards a successful plan for your own promotion. Remember also that work and promotion are not the whole of life. You must decide what part you want them to play in your own life.

2   *Exploit your strengths.* We all have strengths and weaknesses. It is generally more profitable to devote effort to exploiting your strengths than to covering your weaknesses. If you can't add up a row of figures without making a mistake, don't take a job which requires you to do so. If you are forced into such a job get a calulator even if you have to buy it yourself. Protect yourself from your weaknesses either by avoiding unsuitable jobs or by covering your weakness with staff who do not share your weaknesses. Remember that you will be

promoted for your particular strength. If you are strong enough in one thing you will be promoted for this strength in spite of your weaknesses.

3   *Become a jack of all trades and master of one.* Mastery of one skill or specialisation brings you initial promotion. As you move higher up the ladder, particularly if you move into general management, a very broad interest and knowledge of the business is clearly an essential. Too narrow a specialisation limits promotion prospects.

4   *Make your own opportunities.* Some opportunities may be handed to you on a plate. It is more likely that they will not. They will be difficult to recognise and hence many people spend their lives lamenting their lack of opportunities. It is not a matter of luck. You have to plan for your opportunities; you have to create them and you have to be ready to take them. In the words of Ralph Waldo Emerson: 'No great man ever complains of want of opportunity'.

5   *Develop your independence.* No one can be independent if he is up to his ears in debt or if he is tied to one organisation. There are two aspects of independence you should give your mind to if you are ambitious. The first is to develop a degree of financial independence, so that you can afford to take up opportunities when they occur. It also enables you to stick to your views on what is right without that awful worrying feeling about what will happen to you and your family if you lose your job. The second is to develop and keep up to date in your own particular skill and trade. A justified belief in your own ability to do a particular job better than most and the knowledge that you can move almost at will into a similar job elsewhere is the best guarantee of real independence.

6   *Be prepared to take risks.* By this I do not suggest that you should become a gambler. However, certainties are few and far between in this world. Benjamin Franklin went so far as to write: 'In this world nothing can be said to be certain, except death and taxes'. Risks should be carefully evaluated

and you should try to arrange things so that you stand to gain the greatest reward from the lowest possible risk. If you are to get on in life you will have to take some risks. Even crossing a road involves some risk. In the end if you take no risks you will make few mistakes. You will also have at the end of your life, few achievements to your credit.

7   *Be realistic.* Don't deceive yourself about your own strengths and weaknesses. Recognise your own limitations. Where your limitations are serious but can be remedied by training, do something about them. It is enjoyable to dream like Walter Mitty but if you want to progress along the promotion path it is not enough just to dream about it. Make realistic plans and then set about steadily carrying them out.

8   *You can be too clever.* In the real world high levels of intelligence are not always appreciated. The very intelligent man may well be advised to conceal his intelligence below a veneer of sound common sense. It takes most people time to appreciate new ideas. Allow for this. If you have a boss who is a bit slow, don't bombard him with too many fresh ideas, you'll only frighten him. Similarly, if he has a problem which has been worrying him for weeks, it may be tactless to solve it in two minutes flat. In practice the simple solution is normally preferable to the complex one. True cleverness therefore consists in identifying the real problems, asking the right questions and posing simple realistic plans.

9   *Be positive.* Be determined. Be clear about your own plans and objectives. Do not approach them half heartedly. Be determined to achieve what you set out to do. Doubts and feeling that its probably worth a try are a recipe for diasaster. If you have realistically appraised a situation and decided on a plan and on your objectives, go firmly forward to success and do not allow yourself to be discouraged or diverted.

10   *Be resilient.* Always take a positive attitude to your work and your own promotion plans. When you suffer setbacks, as you will, plan and fight your way back. Life is frequently unfair. It does no good to whine about this unfairness when

225

Dont kick anyone on your way up . . .
you may pass them on the way down!

it hits you. Put it down to experience. If you do think about it, do so to find the lessons for the future, not to feel sorry for yourself. Having learnt the lessons, overhaul your plan, set your new objectives and set out with a firm determination to achieve them. Many people in their 40s and 50s feel that a serious setback means the end of their career. It is too late; they feel too old. By contrast, some bounce back and refuse to accept defeat. Perhaps, in the end, only one person can defeat you and that is yourself.

11 *Don't kick anyone you pass on your way up the promotion ladder.* You may pass them again on the way down. If you do find yourself going down for a while, you will find you have very few friends in any organisation. It seems wise to avoid the gratuitous creation of enemies in the days of your success. Generally speaking, it costs nothing to be courteous. Even quite drastic actions can be taken without discourtesy and without kicking anyone. Resist the temptation to throw your weight about as you climb the ladder — it can make it unstable.

12 *Never demand as a right, what you can ask as a favour.* No one likes to face demands. This is particularly true if they know they have to do what is demanded. With no option, the matter and your manner will rankle. On the other hand if you ask politely for a favour it makes the person granting it feel good. He will often feel almost grateful to you and may even come to regard you as a protege.

13 *Keep healthy.* If you are in poor health it will affect your performance. Good health is not just a matter of luck. Admittedly you can be unlucky and suffer a serious accident or disease. Much more ill health, particularly in the middle aged arises from lack of care. Desk-bound jobs, particularly for those who have led active lives before arriving behind a desk, are dangerous. There is a tendency to drive or go by public transport to and from work; to use the lift in the office; and to work such long hours that normal exercise is not taken. This combined with heavy eating soon puts the managers health at risk. Business entertaining is a particular source of danger. When I first had the opportunity of eating at my employer's expense fairly regularly, I used to eat as much as possible. The consequences were soon visible. I cut down by missing out the rolls, butter and sugar. Nowadays I avoid all business eating that I possibly can. Another problem source, however, is the quiet pub lunch with two or three colleagues. Even that can build too much tummy. Moderation in smoking, drinking and eating are likely to contribute greatly to your good health. So too is regular exercise, even if it is only a daily walk or swim. Your health is one of your prime assets — cultivate it.

14 *Speak no evil.* In any organisation, there is a lot of gossip. It is easy enough to tear away at other people's reputation with your tongue. The normal reaction of someone who hears that you have been making slanderous comments about him is that he will reply in kind. Whether his comments are true or not, some of the mud is likely to stick. It is better to keep your views on other people to yourself and to accept them as they are.

15 *Write no evil.* You may sometimes in the course of your work feel that someone has been unhelpful, obstructive, dim, or just a damn fool. It is a mistake to write and tell him so. It is even more unwise to express your view in a clever, witty or sarcastic way. It will rankle. Every time he turns up that memo on the file, his resentment will be rekindled. Unpleasant things are sometimes said just to relieve one's own feelings and frustrations. This is a mistake. There will be however occasions when work demands that unpleasant things must be said. Unless you need a legal record of what is said, it is much better not to write but to say the things face to face. It is not always easy but you make your point with less danger of long run resentment and enmity.

16 *Cherish your boss.* Your future is bound up with his. You can learn a lot from your boss — whether he is a good or bad one. If he does well, he can help you. If he goes steadily to the top, he can take you with him. If your organisation has a formal appraisal or annual review system, it is your boss who will review you. What he writes about you will remain on your file, while you remain with the organisation. But more simply if he is seen as successful, this reputation will rub off on his staff. If he is successful, he has a better chance of securing privileges, salary increases and promotion for his staff. There is a very noticeable difference in your working conditions and prospects if you work for a successful boss as compared with one who is struggling.

17 *Never stab your boss in the back.* It doesn't pay. You remove at a stroke, the man who should be your first champion and advocate in the organisation. If you try but fail to

move him, you will have to move yourself or life will become very uncomfortable. If you succeed you will not necessarily get his job and his successor may be worse. If you get a reputation for treachery, no one will want to have you on their staff. Even the man who encourages you to do the deed will probably disown you and be wary of over-exposing himself to the same fate.

18 *Look after your people.* A manager is dependent on the people who work for him. To do well he has to collect a team who know and can do their job. He has to motivate them to do a good job and to meet their objectives. He is likely to do this most successfully if he looks after them. Make sure that they get the benefits they are entitled to. Ensure they have good working conditions. Don't let anyone else lean on them or push them around. If they are worth promotion try to see they get it. Don't hang on to them to block their career. Your strongest allies in any organisation should be the people you have developed, coached and helped to promotion. This is true even if they overtake you in the race.

19 *Do unto others as you would be done by.* When you do anything try to put yourself in the other person's position. Try to get into his skin and see things from his point of view. If you take action that affects someone else, consider how you would feel if it were done to you. If you would feel that it was unfair, then refrain from doing it to someone else.

20 *Be lucky in your choice of wife and take the time and trouble to establish and maintain a firm home base.* A secure, tension-free home provides a good starting point for any manager. So too, does the right wife, who can cope with the many exigencies of the promotion path. Bouncing back from adversity or even coping with redundancy is much easier for the man with a happy wife and home.

21 *Recognise your own motives.* When you decide on a certain course of action, be clear about your own motives. It is foolish to conceal them from yourself. Recognise your own greed and ambition. You do not have to say goodbye

to your principles and ideals if you set out to climb the
promotion ladder. Indeed you will probably find it easier
to live with yourself if you stick to your principles.

> *'This above all: to thine own self be true;*
> *And it must follow, as the night the day,*
> *Thou canst not then be false to any man.*
> *Farewell. My blessing season this in thee!'*

Bibliography

Anstey, E., *Committees: How they work and how to work them,* Allen & Unwin (1965).

Argyle, M., *Social interactions,* Penguin (1969).

Burger, N.H., *The executive's wife,* Collier Books (1968).

Buzan, Tony, *Speed reading,* Sphere (1970).

Buzan, Tony, *Speed memory,* Sphere (1971).

Chandor, A., *Choosing and keeping computer staff,* George Allen & Unwin (1976).

Dempsey, P.J.R. *Psychology and the manager,* Pan (1973).

De Leeuw, M., and De Leeuw, E., *Read better and faster,* Pelican (1965).

Dixon, N.F., *On the psychology of military incompetence,* Cape (1976).

Drucker, P.F., *The effective executive,* Pan (1967).

Drucker, P.F., *The age of discontinuity,* Pan (1969).

Drucker, P.F., *The practise of management,* Mercury Books (1961).

Drucker, P.F., *Managing for results,* Heinemann, 1964

Dunnette, M.D., *Personnel selection and placement,* Tavistock Publications (1966).

Emery, F.E. (Editor), *Systems thinking* Penguin (1969).

Geoffman, E., *Presentation of the self in everyday life,* Penguin (1971).

Gowers, Sir Ernest, *The complete plain words* HMSO (1973).

Hague, H., *Executive self-development*, Macmillan (1974).

Humble, J., *Improving business results ,* Pan (1972).

231

Leigh, A., *You and your job,* Oxford University Press (1971).

Lewis, R., and Stewart, R., *The boss,* Phoenix (1961).

Lupton, Tom, *Management and the social sciences*, Penguin (1966).

Machiavelli, *The Prince,* Penguin (1961).

Machorton, Ian, *How to get a better job in management,* Mercury House (1971).

Moreau, David, *Look behind you,* Associated Book Programs (1973).

Packard, Vance, *The pyramid climbers,* Longmans, Green (1972).

Peter, L.J., and Hull, R., *The Peter Principle,* Pan (1970).

Proxy, G., *How to get your boss's job* Pitman (1970).

Puckey, Sir Walter, *Management principles,* Hutchinson (1962).

Reddin, W.J., *Managerial effectiveness,* McGraw Hill (1970).

Robens, Lord, *Human engineering*, Jonathon Cape (1970).

Rowntree, Derek, *Learn how to study,* Macdonald (1970).

Scanlan, Burt. K., *Principles of management and organisational behaviour,* John Wiley, (1973).

Sidney, E., Brown, M., and Argyle, M., *Skills with people,* Hutchinson (1973).

Silverman, David, *The theory of organisations,* Heinemann (1970).

Stewart, R., *The reality of organisations: a guide for managers,* Macmillan (1970).

Taylor, W.J., and Watling, T.F., *The basic arts of management,* Business Books (1972).

Taylor, W.J., and Watling, T.F., *Successful project management,* Business Books (1970).

Taylor, W.J. and Watling, T.F., *Practical project management,* Halstead Press & Business Books (1973).

Taylor, W.J. and Watling, T.F., *Personal finance for managers,* Business Books (1972).

Tillett, T., Kempner, T., and Wills, G. (Editors), *Management thinkers,* Penguin (1970).

Vroom, V.H., and Deci, E.L., *Management and motivation,* Penguin (1970).

Watling, T.F., and Morley, J.D., *Successful commodity futures trading,* Business Books (1974).

Index

professional firm, 99
See also, Qualifications
Speed Memory, 171
Speed Reading, 170
Sport, 210-11
Staff:
    central, 148-9
    index, 118
    rotation, 201
Staleness, 9-10, 20, 31, 44
    See also, Restlessness
Status/symbols, 5-7, 45-6
    and demotion, 220
    and graduates, 63, 69
    and Peter Principle, 82
    and specialists, 83
    in bureaucracies, 102
Subsidiary company, 75, 98, 100
Successful Project Management, 192
Swift, Dean Jonathan, 38, 147
Systems designer, *see* Specialists

Taylor, Sir Henry, 221, 222
Taylor, John, 192, 199, 210
Technical books, 200, 205
Technical journals, 101
    See also, Press
Thomas, Leslie, 166
Thurber, James, 89
To a Mouse, 13
Trade association, 191
Trade journals, 106, 169, 200, 205
    See also, Press
Trade unions, 26, 28, 55, 73

imposing constraints, 154
in family firms, 106
negotiation with, 174
Training/trainees, 29-30, 71, 73-6, 77-8, 98
    courses, 14, 21, 99, 200
    day-release, 99
    evening-classes, 99
    formal system, 118
    for misfits, 7, 220-1
    for specialists, 62, 99
    for your own staff, 201
    graduates, 67, 118
    in mid-career, 7, 10, 222
learning by doing, 74, 75
    management, 27
    manuals, 50
    needed for promotion, 108, 122, 225
Transfers *see* Interdepartmental movement
Tropic of Ruislip, 166

Unilever, 28
Univac, 28
University/ies, 9, 63, 78
    business schools, 99
    See also, Open University

Voluntary redundancy, 220

Wife/ves, 45, 165, 213, 229
    See also, Family life
Writing, 50, 174-7, 192